7 HEAVENLY HABITS OF INNOVATION

Mat Shore | OUTSIDEIN

CONTENTS
7 Heavenly Habits of Innovation

Heavenly Habits and Deadly Sins – The Infographic 3
Introduction – What Myself and Rob Lowe Have In Common 4
The Faster Horse Myth 6
Why No-one is Perfect 8
Habit 1. Focus and Move the Mouse 10
         Heavenly Case Study – Lego Friends 12
         Hellish Case Study – Nokia Hair Coach. 14
Habit 2. Ask a Different Question 16
         Heavenly Case Study –EcoHelmet 18
         Hellish Case Study – MoviePass 20
Habit 3. Throw One Ball 22
         Heavenly Case Study- Mom Inflatable Incubator 24
         Hellish Case Study – Dyson Hairdyer. 26
Habit 4. Happy to Hear No! 28
         Heavenly Case Study – Apple Newton, Bubble Wrap, WebOS . . . 30
         Hellish Case Study – Tidal Music Streaming 32
Habit 5. Hide the Hero. 34
         Heavenly Case Study – Patek Phillipe 36
         Hellish Case Study – Nike HyperAdapt 2.0 38
Habit 6. Bounce Just Once 40
         Heavenly Case Study – Samsung FlexWash & AddWash. 42
         Hellish Case Study – Juicero. 44
Habit 7. Look Down the Chain 46
         Heavenly Case Study – Magic Mirrors. 48
         Hellish Case Study - UbaMarket 50
And Finally.. Some More Heavenly Examples. 52
The 6 Elements Method 54
About Mat Shore. 55
Booking Outside In 56
Jargon Buster – Mat's Innovation Dictionary 58

Copyright © 2017 by Mathew Shore

All rights reserved. This book or any portion thereof may not be reproduced or used in any manner whatsoever physical or digital without the express written permission of Mathew Shore except for the use of brief quotations in a book review.
This book contains tools and techniques including the 7 Heavenly Habits of Innovation and the 6 Blocker design and wording which are the copyright of Mat Shore Ltd and may not be replicated or used without permission of the owners. No transfer of ownership is given or inferred through inclusion in this book.

Printed in the United Kingdom
This edition 2017

Mat Shore LTD
28 Abbey Road, Chertsey, KT16 8AL
www.MatShore.com
matshore@matshore.com
Subscribe to Mats' YouTube Channel:
MatShoreInnovation

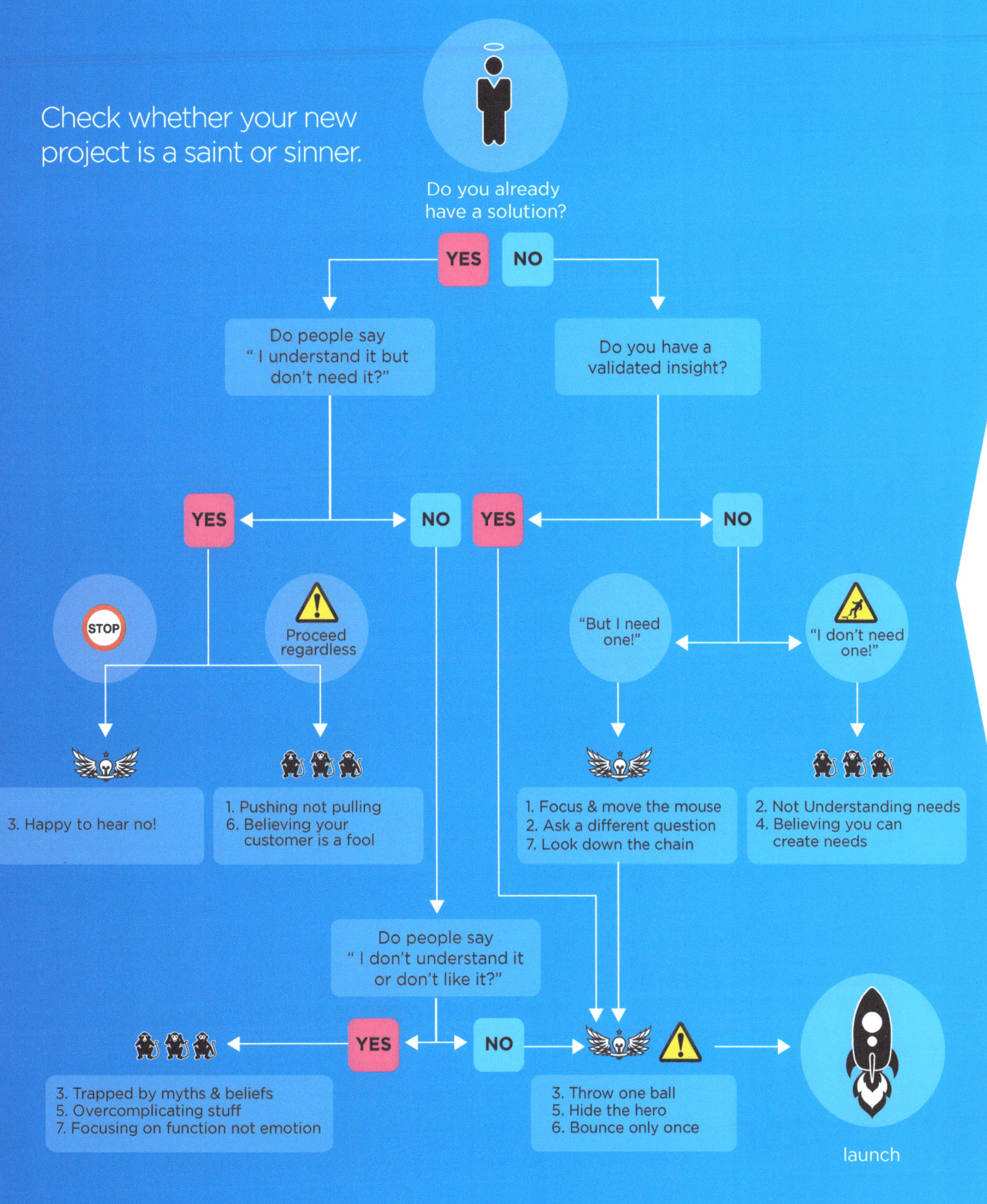

INTRODUCTION

What myself and Rob Lowe have in common
(Or how I ended up practicing what I preach)

Creating a great Value Proposition is about narrowing down your offer and then repeating it so relentlessly that your target can't help but associate it with you.

As usual I'd like to start with a story. I started my career in brand management at Procter & Gamble, Pepsi and Unilever and towards the end of my time there I was unhappy in my role. I no longer wanted to be a jack of all trades, instead I wanted to specialise in the early stages of innovation; it was where my passion and strengths lay.

One day I ended up in a meeting with HR. Less a meeting really, more a showdown.

HR were trying to rationalise with me that if I stuck at it, focused on the areas I disliked, broadened my competencies, I could one day hope to be general manager of Venezuela. Don't get me wrong, I've nothing against Venezuela per say, it's just that I didn't want to be a general manager. This was the part that seemed to be stumping my employer!

"Why wouldn't you want to be a generalist, running all aspects and functions of the organisation?" they asked.

"Because I want to be a specialist," I replied, "focusing on one thing and known for doing it really, really well."

"We don't need people like that," came the response. "They are hard to manage, need moving more frequently and tend to become bored quickly."

A pretty fair summation of me, as anyone who knows me will attest.

So it was that I was compelled by necessity to leave the corporate world and start up my own business: training and consultancy company called Outside In.

In the early days as the work began to evolve and positive word of mouth grew around my insight and Value Proposition training, I was asked to train other things.

PowerPoint for beginners, finance for non-financial managers and time management, amongst other things.

I stuck to my convictions that if you specialise at something, then you start to stand for something. If you try to be a jack of all trades, then you risk standing for nothing. As a result I rejected all offers of work that weren't directly related to the development of innovation and Value Propositions Turning down real paying work in order to maintain strategic consistency takes nerves of steel and there were times my resolve began to wobble! But I stuck at it.

As time went on and I refined my own company's target, I narrowed yet further to working only with complex technology companies and science and engineering driven organisations. I decided this was an area which required unique solutions and where I could have a discriminated offer.

Each time my target became smaller, the resonance of what I did became more pronounced. I started to get calls from new clients along the lines of "I hear that you are the only one that does this", or "I've moved to a new company which is technology driven too, don't change anything, just say what you said last time."

Far from losing work, as my target and Value Proposition has narrowed my brand has grown.

And what of Rob Lowe, you may quite reasonably ask?

A few years ago I went to see Rob Lowe (he of 1980s Brat Pack fame) at the opening night of a West End version of 'A Few Good Men'. He was outstanding and as the big star name on the stage, most people in the audience had gone specifically to see him.

About a year later I was reading the London Evening Standard and saw an advert that read: "Rob Lowe, still going strong in 'A Few Good Men'!". A year later, 7 days a week, plus 2 matinees, Rob Lowe was still delivering the same script and performance on stage, his passion for the role undiminished.

Soon my company will reach its 15th anniversary; in that time I'll have trained tens of thousands of people all around the world on just this one subject. As with Rob Lowe, it's required a hell of a lot of repetition (sometimes I dream my presentation in my sleep!), but just like my Heavenly Habit 1 – 'Focus and Move the Mouse', and Habit 3 – 'Throw One Ball', even though my target is narrow and my offer is too, there's a lot of demand for repeat performances.

In this book I will endeavour to share with you the 7 Heavenly Habits that are essential to ensuring you can make great innovation that is discriminated and targeted. Enjoy the ride.

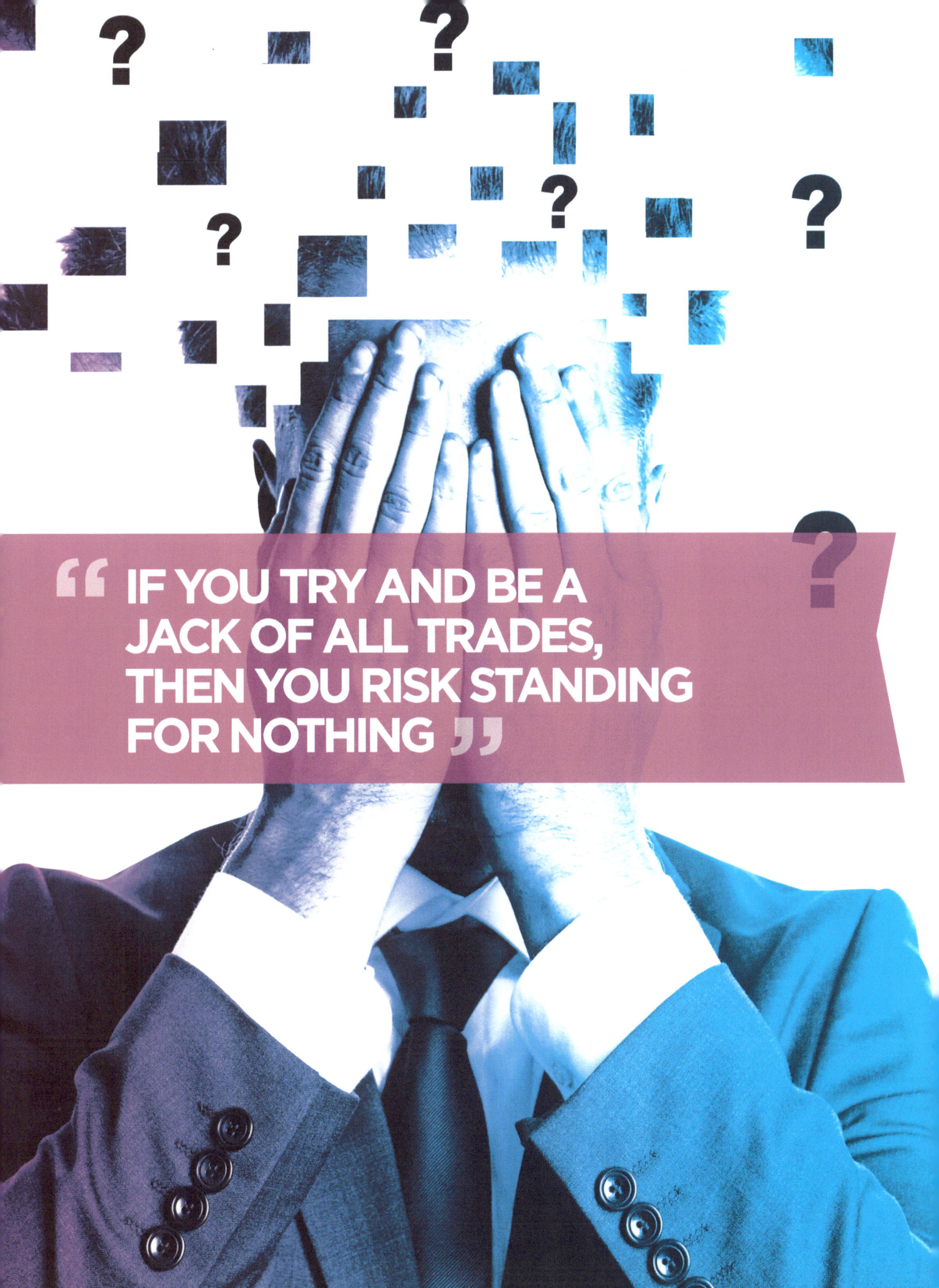

THE FASTER HORSE MYTH
Or how some try to deny the need for Customer Insight

The essence of all Heavenly Innovation is the use of customer and consumer insight to determine whether there is a need for the solution being proposed.

It's known as insight driven innovation and it's the cornerstone of everything you will read in this book. However, there remains a vocal contingent who deny that asking customers what they need is useful, helpful or even possible. They use a famous quote by Ford to support their assertion.

If you are one of the few that isn't aware of the quote I'm referring to then the story is as follows. When asked why he didn't ask consumers what they needed, Ford is reputed to have said, "If I'd have asked them what they needed, they would have said a faster horse.". QED.

- Consumers and customers cannot be trusted as the basis of informed innovation because they don't know what they don't know.
- Market research is a waste of money, pour the funds into engineering and R&D budgets instead.
- Customers and consumers will only answer you based on their limited understanding of what is currently available and cannot possibly be expected to give you an educated response based on technological shifts or disruptions they have no visibility on.

Codswallop!

This approach to consumer insight denial has fed legions of engineers, product managers and 'entrepreneurs' over the years ignoring their customer and consumer on the basis that they know better.

This quote is the foundation stone of what I call 'Technology Push', the extremely unreliable and risky method of creating innovations and technologies immune from fear that no one needs them.

Technology Push is an evangelic approach to customer needs that is driven by the mistaken belief that once the customer sees how clever you have been, they will discover they need you after all.

Most companies (particularly big companies with sizeable R&D spends) have an atrocious hit rate on innovation success vs failure. However these are exactly the companies where self-belief in the power of technology to make needs appear miraculously out of the ether is at its strongest.

"The consumer would never have asked for the internet!" is the supporting statement.

QED. The consumer didn't know that the internet was possible, so clearly wouldn't have asked for it in advance.

Are you insane?

Of course the consumer wouldn't have asked for the internet because the internet is not a need! No one goes through life thinking, "You know what I need right now, an internet!"

It enables benefits to be offered. It is not in itself a benefit! Always remember, apart from a super elite of techno geeks, most people buy what something does, not how it does it!

If you look at every big success of the internet age, they didn't create new needs, they solved existing needs (to fall in love, to trade better, to know the status of your friend's relationships better). They happened to use the internet as an enabler.

Look at this chart. People are booking taxis quicker, watching films more conveniently, finding an appropriate date more effectively. They are not buying the internet; that's there in the background but not the point.

The question Ford posed is flawed because it required the respondent to redesign the solution, not describe the desired outcome. The drill not the hole!

What do those who throw this quote around expect to have happened? Ford: "How can we improve your horse?"

Consumer: "Have you got a pencil?"

I hope you get all this down! You're going to need to develop a thing called an internal combustion engine, then what I want you to do is build a mass production capability. Are you getting this?"

How nutty is that approach? Just because the target doesn't understand the technology doesn't mean they don't understand the need.

What should Ford have asked?

"Forget the horse for a second, tell me what your desired outcome is and let me worry about how that's done."

Now that quote enables creativity!

It enables brilliant entrepreneurship and creativity in engineering!

But it does so in the full knowledge of what is needed and gives the organisation confidence that when it's done, there will be a market!

The 7 Heavenly Habits of Innovation involve seeking to understand problems better and reverse the culture in many technology companies that the customer doesn't know what they need.

If you have team members who use the Ford quote a bit too often to avoid market research or basing their solutions on customer needs, show them this book and point them in my direction.

> **JUST BECAUSE THE TARGET DOESN'T UNDERSTAND THE TECHNOLOGY DOESN'T MEAN THEY DON'T UNDERSTAND THE NEED**

BRAND	PER MINUTE	PRE-EXISTING NEED:
UBER	1,500 Rides	To catch a taxi home and know you have a means to pay
NETFLIX	69,444 hours watched	To watch a wider selection of movies and TV at home
tinder	972,222 swipes	To find and date someone that's a better match without being rejected
Spotify	38,052 hours of music	To listen to more of your favourite music at home or on the go
amazon	$230,000 in sales	To buy things more conveniently after drinking wine late at night
facebook	700,000 log ins	To gossip easier and find out whether your friends have split up
Google	2.4 million searches	To search for information more simply and become better educated.

WHY NO-ONE IS PERFECT

And so this book has good and bad case studies

My first book was snappily entitled 'The 7 Deadly Sins of Innovation' and was published 2 years ago.

Within its colourful pages were case study after case study of catastrophically bad innovation that was poorly conceived and often hilariously executed. These awards for ill-thought-out ideas were not exclusively reserved for small companies and products like the internet connected egg tray and the doomed Air Umbrella, but large corporations spending billions, such as the case of the Apple Watch.

In the years since I wrote about these case studies, the majority have gone bust and lost their designers and investors a heap of money. The Apple Watch may still be limping along at the time of writing, but as with most wearable manufacturers the company is desperately trying to encourage people to carry on charging and using the device after the initial 3-month honeymoon period. Tellingly, Apple fails to discuss in any meaningful detail the performance of this major launch even 2 years after launch, which you'd expect them to do if it had been the success they were expecting.

Over the years since the book came out, many people have asked me why I don't write a companion piece on good innovation. Lovely case studies that focus on the positive and show what happens when things go right. A book full of rainbows and ponies, the business book equivalent of a warm, soothing bowl of chicken soup.

This, I thought, was a good insight.

However, it wasn't a quantitatively validated insight.

Thus I set about building an online blog at MatShore.com where I regularly publish new case studies and run them through my 6 Element Value Proposition approach to analyse the insight and the clarity of the idea. Social media sites such as LinkedIn, Facebook, Quora and Twitter have proven to be a great way to share regular case studies of good and bad innovation. Some of those blogs have received upwards of 10,000 people reading them and my YouTube channel MatShoreInnovation has 75,000 views. So we know people like reading my case studies, but here's what's interesting when you correlate the results.

Examples of good innovation get a healthy numbers of views, but examples of abysmal innovation get more. Vastly more.

That of course is an observation not an insight!

Here's my hypothesis on why that might be.

Either I've surrounded myself entirely with a network of cynics, who expect me to find the hilarious bad case studies and look forward to a right-regal, no holds barred, tongue-in-cheek deconstruction. This could be true, as I now have an army of helpful souls who forward me all sorts of crazy inventions and products for inclusion in my blog every month.

Or, in general we don't like to be told that anyone is perfect and even when we see good examples, we want to know that there is balance in the universe and crap stuff happens too.

As my inner Chi craves balance, I have resolved to strike that equilibrium within this book.

Therefore, although the book is entitled 'The 7 Heavenly Habits of Innovation', you will find that for each habit I have sought out both a good and bad example. A case study that demonstrates what happens when the correct thinking is applied and a counterpoint that shows the darker, seedier underbelly of innovation.

Hell, it makes for a more entertaining read after all!

Onwards then to our first habit...

> "WE WANT TO KNOW THAT THERE IS BALANCE IN THE UNIVERSE AND CRAP STUFF HAPPENS TOO"

HABIT 1

FOCUS & MOVE THE MOUSE

Why there is no such thing as a Universal Insight

When people ask me how to gain better customer insight, I tell them there are just 2 ways.

Firstly, you can ask a different person and secondly, you can ask a different question.

Habit 1 – 'Focus & Move the Mouse' concerns itself with the first of these variables, whilst Habit 2 – 'Ask a Different Question' covers the latter.

At the heart of a good Product Idea is the need to define the customer pain before you can be sure your solution will create value. Yet every year I coach and critique the creation of thousands of Value Propositions where teams can't find that compelling insight.

In many cases that's because their target is too large. They delude themselves they're creating a solution that will be attractive for everyone! At least you can't fault their ambition!

It's a confusion between target and business case that makes them aim as broad as possible so they can project huge potential rewards and convince key stakeholders to back their project. Of course, it's false economy! For value to be created, a salient problem must be identified and solved. Vague and diverse targets have vague and diverse problems. On the other hand, clearly segmented targets share common needs, priorities and collective beliefs.

Many years ago, when I was interviewed for my innovation role at Unilever, they only asked me one question. Is there such a thing as a Universal Insight? I know why they asked that question, because it's the killer dichotomy at the heart of marketing.

Wouldn't it be convenient if everyone in the world shared the same need, same priorities, same attitudes? Hell, then we could make one solution to fit everyone, save money on R&D, logistics, packaging, communication. No need for regional or local teams, just a single Value Proposition appealing to a universal audience.

Unfortunately, I had to burst that particular bubble and say there are no such things as Universal Insights,. and that all unmet needs are target dependent and context dependent.

Let me demonstrate my point. Imagine I'm trying to define the key insight for a new car. I make my target everyone in the world and now I'm striving to find that illusive Universal Insight. Can I safely assume that everyone wants a car to be safe or fast or spacious?

What if I needed to be more specific to allow R&D to focus on relevant features? Maybe I'd start by focusing on the safety of the children in the back. But hang on! Not everyone has kids so I can't focus around child safety, because that would be irrelevant to a large proportion of my target.

What about passenger safety? No, not everyone drives with a passenger. Off road ability? No, same problem.

It becomes clear that without making significant choices about who you are solving for, you can't make any clear identification of the relevant pain points or compromises that need to be overcome.

I was once in Germany training a large group of PHDs who worked on theoretical technologies in an R&D department (tough gig right?). One of the scientists told me that at Berkley University they did a study to see when a cat pounces on a mouse. If the mouse stayed still, the cat did nothing; only if it moved did the cat spring into action.

"We don't want dead mouse insights where our customer does nothing!" said the scientist. "We need moving mouse insights", "How do we generate insights where the customer is compelled to act?" This probably remains one of the best questions I've been asked from any of my 35,000 trainees.

The answer is simple. We need to narrow the target. By narrowing the target, we know not only who we are trying to create value for, but also who we don't need to satisfy. Only once we know this can we solve their priority insights without constant fear of alienating and disenfranchising others.

Only by abandoning the illusion of a Universal Insight and narrowing the target can we truly hope to become relevant and differentiated enough to move that mouse.

 **Great innovators create solutions that are uniquely relevant to only a segment of the market when others try and fail to appeal to everyone.**

> "ONLY BY ABANDONING THE ILLUSION OF A UNIVERSAL INSIGHT AND NARROWING THE TARGET CAN WE TRULY HOPE TO BECOME RELEVANT AND DIFFERENTIATED ENOUGH TO MOVE THAT MOUSE"

LEGO FRIENDS

Focus & Move the Mouse

One of my favourite innovations of the last few years is Lego Friends, the new range of construction toys designed exclusively for girls.

When it first came to market there were howls of derision from the usual suspects that think that anything targeted at girls is inherently sexist. Presumably they believe that there should be no targeting at all and that everyone of all genders should think alike, act alike and need exactly the same things.

Don't get me wrong, there are colossally stupid innovations offered to girls, such as the recent Clarks kids' shoes debacle in which they produced exactly the same design of shoes for boys and girls. Unfortunately they positioned the boys' shoes as 'Leader Play' and the girls' shoes as 'Dolly Babe'. The resulting outcry led to the shoes being unceremoniously pulled from sale and Clarks apologised for any unintended offense caused.

Lego had historically been guilty of the same thinking by making construction sets for girls which were roughly identical to the ones for boys but were pink, such as the pastel-shaded disaster that was the Paradisa range in the 1990s. The approach of creating a 'one size fits all' set of bricks with superficial naming and branding differences wasn't working.

Thus it was in 2008 that Lego began to look properly at the girl market for the first time. They narrowed their focus and were able to ask deeper, richer questions of the target audience. It took them 4 years of insight and proposition development before they were ready to launch in January 2012.

So what did they learn by talking to the target using sophisticated market research techniques?

Well, they learned that boys and girls think about construction toys differently. Boys have pirate sets, space sets, city sets and these are populated by an extensive assortment of spacemen, pirates and city dwellers, just as you'd expect.

The key thing is, boys don't care what they are called! They don't want to know that this is Dave the policeman, that he has 3 kids, a wife and a dog and he's friends with Barry the fireman. Nope, they just think about him as a minifigure.

Lego's research found that girls think differently. They don't want hundreds of nameless, faceless characters. If the worlds they create are populated by anyone, then they need to know their names, their complete backstory, their friendships, their likes/dislikes. In fact, for girls having less characters is desirable, but having more developed personalities is essential.

That's why Lego Friends is a town (Heartlake City) built around only 5 characters: Mia, Olivia, Andrea, Stephanie and Emma. The different interests of the girls are reflected in the unique Lego sets they are included in and are meant to help a girl find a character whose interests identify with her own. These personalities and relationships are further explored in videos online, storybooks and social media platforms making Lego Friends transcend just the core construction toy and become a multi-faceted way for Lego to engage with the target.

The researchers at Lego also discovered that boys only really care about the exteriors of the things they build. Sure it's a police station or an intergalactic star destroyer, but what's the décor like on the inside? Who cares?

Girls do!

Girls are highly engaged by both the interiors and exteriors of the buildings that they create. If there is a coffee shop, it needs to have tiny accurate details from cupcakes to cappuccino machines; the veterinarian clinic will have all the necessary equipment to euthanise that show pony if required. It's why the Lego Friends proposition has come together, when previous attempts to simply take the boy product and paint it pink had failed.

And how has it done?

There are two measures of success we can take. Firstly, the business results. According to Fortune magazine, Lego's success among girls can be seen in the market for girls' construction toys in the U.S. and the larger European countries, which tripled to $900 million in just two years after its launch in 2012, according to research firm NPD Group. This increase is believed to be due to the entry of Lego Friends.

The other measure is the effect on my 4 boys. Near my house is Legoland Windsor, which used to have a large construction area complete with fully working vehicles called 'Digger Land'.

Last year, to the great disgust of my boys, Digger Land was unceremoniously demolished and replaced by Lego Friends Heartlake City. "There are loads more girls at Legoland nowadays," one of them told me last time we visited.

Well done Lego, seems like you've focused and moved that mouse.

> "THE APPROACH OF CREATING A 'ONE SIZE FITS ALL' SET OF BRICKS WITH SUPERFICIAL NAMING AND BRANDING DIFFERENCES WASN'T WORKING"

CASE STUDY

NOKIA HAIR BRUSH

Focus & Move the Mouse

Time after time, fad after fad, there is somebody who tries to justify the irrelevance of their innovation by riding on the coat-tails of a fashionable technology. Normally this trendy technology platform is shoe-horned into their Value Proposition to appeal to the terminally gullible hipsters of the world or the equally shallow venture capital community.

One such trendy technology coat-tail at the moment is the Internet of Things (IOT).

As I may have said once or twice previously, I'm not a big believer that the Internet of Things has a Value Proposition. Just like the internet that came before it, IOT is an enabler to other solutions that still need to have relevance by solving unmet needs in their own right.

You can't justify a pointless innovation with the simple defence of "It must be useful, it's part of the Internet of Things". Pointless is still pointless in my book.

Nonetheless, a quick review of recent innovations in the arena of IOT provides a salutary lesson that when it comes to innovation the blind still lead the blind. You can get an internet connected diaper to tell you when your baby's pooped. I tend to use the old method of holding its bum close to my nose as this avoids the risk of my baby's arse inadvertently becoming disconnected from the server! You can get internet connected wine bottles, vacuum cleaners and bird houses, along with fire alarm batteries, toothbrushes and razor blades.

The best (worst) example of this dumb quest to make things smart (apologies for the triple oxymoron) is the Nokia Hair Coach which in essence is an IOT connected hair brush.

As if to try and spread the blame for this pointless innovation as broadly and as widely as possible the hair brush in question seems to come from 4 brands. It was developed by Withings, which is a subsidiary of Nokia, in association with L'Oreal's innovation lab and Kerastase, one of L'Oreal's premium hair care brands.

Seems like no one here really wants to own up and take the blame for this!

And what exactly is the Hair Coach?

Well, it's a Wi-Fi enabled, Bluetooth equipped hair brush that helps you look after your hair by providing an inordinate amount of useless data sent to an app on your phone (highly likely you'll not be receiving this information on a Nokia phone as their record on relevant innovation has somewhat let them down recently!).

And how does the smart hair brush know whether you are looking after your hair appropriately? I'm glad you asked that. According to the manufacturers it 'listens' to your hair-brushing patterns using a microphone. Yes you heard that right (as did your brush, apparently).

It combines this aural analysis with an accelerometer and a gyroscope, commodity sensors and transducers that measure the pressure you are applying to your hair, whether your hair is wet or dry when you brush and how much damage you are doing. This is then sent to an app on your phone which provides insights into manageability, frizziness, dryness, split ends and breakage (I don't want to be pedantic but they are more like observations than insights!). The app records the treatment you have doled out to your follicles in case the hair police ever need to take further action.

Of course being wirelessly connected and crammed full of more high tech sensors than an average Mars probe, the Hair Coach will chew through batteries and is somewhat heavier than your average brush.

Maybe the most self-defeating part of the proposition is that when I tell you the brush costs upwards of $200 it will probably make your hair fall out anyway! Have the designers really demonstrated Habit 1 – 'Focus & Move the Mouse'? Have they identified a clear segmentation and narrowed down to understand their real needs?

Let's imagine for a second that Nokia and L'Oreal have a target in mind for their internet connected Smart Hair Brush, who would that be? Someone who can't tell if their hair is tangled, can't tell how long they've been brushing, can't tell if their hair is wet or dry...oh and must have more money than sense.

Does that sound like you? Well roll right up then for the Withings/ Nokia/L'Oreal/ Kerastase Hair Coach.

> "YOU CAN'T JUSTIFY A POINTLESS INNOVATION WITH THE SIMPLE DEFENCE OF "IT MUST BE USEFUL, IT'S PART OF THE INTERNET OF THINGS". POINTLESS IS STILL POINTLESS IN MY BOOK"

HABIT 2

ASK A DIFFERENT QUESTION
Why the truly curious ask new questions five times

About 10 years ago I was a keynote speaker at a large innovation forum in Malmo, Sweden. At the end of the program there was an expert Q&A panel with questions opened to the audience. Someone asked, "How do I make my organisation more insightful?" and a panel member sitting next to me on stage responded with a fascinating answer. He replied, "You can't, you either recruit curious people or you don't."

I guess what the panellist was implying was that if you pick the right people to run your insight projects it's not just the process and tools employed, but their personality and empathy that will determine the quality of results.

This isn't a trait unique to any particular function, I've found just as many marketing people as engineers who do everything within their power to avoid engaging with their customer and think they already know it all.

On the other hand, these people have counterparts who are fascinated by why customers think what they think and do what they do. They are passionately curious about digging into trends and patterns of customer behaviour to understand what's going on below the surface.

However, even the most curious individuals fall into the trap of asking the same old questions unless they are trained to approach customer interviews differently and are armed with the tools to ask better questions.

As I said in the previous habit, there are just 2 ways to improve your insight generation.

Firstly, you can ask a different person and secondly, you can ask a different question.

I've talked extensively in 'The 7 Deadly Sins of Innovation' about the drill vs the hole, an analogy which explains how a question can be predicated on the assumption that the customer needs a technology rather than a benefit.

Switching questions from closed questions in which the customer can only answer yes or no such as "Do you like these Apple EarPods?" to the desired outcome "How do you tend to listen to music?" and "Where else would you like to be able to listen to music but can't now?" are a great start.

What is certain is, asking the same customer the same question that you've been asking for 20 years is pretty futile. The definition of insanity is repeating the same actions over and over again and expecting different results.

This cycle of asking the same people the same questions and getting the same old answers is how companies eventually justify the conclusion they already know it all. Too frequently I consult at companies where the perception of market research is toxic because they never hear anything they don't already know! Not only that but because they are asking the same questions to the same people as their competitors, they gain no competitive advantage.

There's a simple technique called the 5 Whys which helps those with an innate curiosity to dig deeper into the customer's unmet needs and underlying motivations. It works like this.

When you first ask a customer what they think or why they behave in a certain way, the chances are that their response will be incorrect or incomplete. Not because they are lying to you or want you to solve the wrong issues, but inherently because their first response is a 'throw-away' quick-fire answer designed to see how interested you really are.

Perhaps they also haven't given it much thought themselves and so this is their own superficial summation of the situation. "Why do you brush your teeth in cold water?", "Because I've always done it that way", or "Because my mum and dad taught me to do it that way".

The 5 Whys encourages us never to accept the first answer as gospel but to go further and to ask additional questions. This process of digging deeper into the thought processes and behaviour of our customer requires us to find weaknesses and inconsistencies in each subsequent response and to use those to tease out the real answers.

As Monty Python might have said, if you want to find fresh, competitive insights you need to challenge and build in this way not once, not twice, thou must count to five. Five shall be the number of the counting and the number of the counting shall be five. Four shalt thou not count. Six is right out!

It's vital to be curious and empathetic when creating insights, but it's equally important to ask questions in a different way if you intend to learn something new.

 Great innovators learn fresh customer insights by asking a different question or asking questions in a different way.

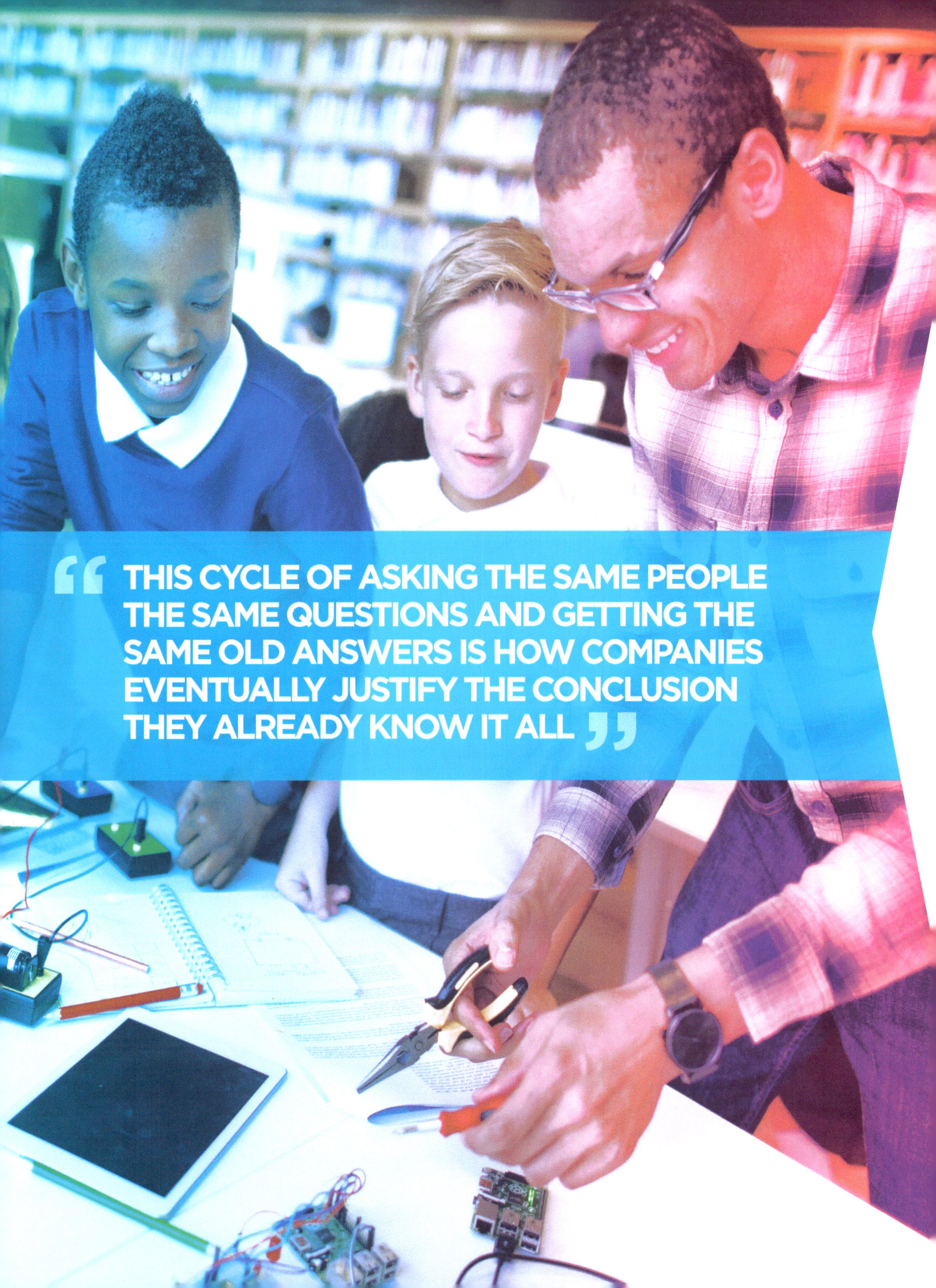

> "THIS CYCLE OF ASKING THE SAME PEOPLE THE SAME QUESTIONS AND GETTING THE SAME OLD ANSWERS IS HOW COMPANIES EVENTUALLY JUSTIFY THE CONCLUSION THEY ALREADY KNOW IT ALL"

ECOHELMET
Ask a Different Question

I always ask teams that are developing insights to start with observations, trends and patterns of behaviour. We can always synthesise these into insights later by asking deeper questions and build credible Value Propositions, but without interesting facts and curious statistics where would we start?

This case study began in exactly that way, when 28-year-old industrial designer Isis Shiffer observed the steady increase in the popularity of bike sharing among those living in cities and towns. From the US to China to the UK, the number of people bike sharing or hiring bikes for short journeys has sky rocketed. In London alone the Boris Bikes (named after the Edwardian Style renowned international diplomat who instigated the scheme) recorded 100,000 hires in a single day.

But Isis observed something equally significant: that for those millions of users, there is no easy way to rent a helmet.

That means that unless all those users turn up prepared with their own helmet then it's highly likely they are riding around with their heads unprotected on some of the world's most congested and dangerous roads.

So we know what people are doing and why they are doing it, but what's the solution?

Well, Isis proposed a one-use only, disposable helmet that you could purchase from a vending machine at the nearest bike share station and that conveniently pop in the recycle bin when you complete your journey.

She named the helmet 'EcoHelmet' which in all fairness it is, but I think underplays the core discriminator of the Value Proposition which is the stunning convenience and the spontaneous one-use benefit. A naming session might be in order here before the final product comes to market I think.

The helmet costs just $5 which post-Brexit could be around £500 (again, thanks Boris).

So we're clear on the benefit, it's an impulse purchase that can protect you as well as normal cycle helmet, but costs a fraction of the price and is entirely disposable.

So what is the explanation for how the helmet is convenient and disposable?

Well it's made from paper you see, which can be folded up to the size of a banana making it ultra-portable and convenient in a vending machine and carried round ready for use before being recycled.

Sounds convenient, but doesn't sound safe?

It is here within the Value Proposition that Isis needed to be crystal clear on the 'Reasons to Believe' (RTB), as my mind is sceptical as to how that could be achieved.

According to the designer: "The EcoHelmet features a radial honeycomb pattern that absorbs a hard blow and spreads impact evenly around the head making it as safe as an established helmet design. The paper is coated with a corn-based biodegradable wax that makes it waterproof -- the same kind that coats disposable coffee cups."

When critiquing Value Propositions within my clinics I always respond to RTBs like that by saying "You would say that wouldn't you?" "..but what evidence have you that it actually works in practice?"

The designer appears to have that covered, she's clearly asked the target what they need, what they expect, what they are worried about, what evidence they would need. She seems to have covered the 5 Whys comprehensively.

To answer those concerns about real life efficacy the designer tested it by using a crash test set up. "We dropped 10 pounds of weight from 3 feet and it withstood the impact," she said.

The helmet has undergone tests which will ensure it safely passes US federal safety standards before it comes to market.

The helmet has won a number of awards including beating 99 other entrants in the James Dyson Award in 2016 . Perhaps Isis could explain to James how he might also make relevant cost effective solutions of his own (see my Dyson Hairdryer Case Study on page 26 to see what I mean).

What I like most about the EcoHelmet is the clarity of the insight on which it is based, clearly having been derived from fully understanding the needs of bike sharers and the unique issues that they face in balancing safety and convenience.

There could also be many other applications for a one use only or portable safety helmet, from building sites and factories to rock climbing and potholing. Isis now needs to look at different markets, and continue her passion for asking different questions.

> **"THE INSIGHT IS DERIVED FROM FULLY UNDERSTANDING THE NEEDS OF BIKE SHARERS AND THE UNIQUE ISSUES THAT THEY FACE IN BALANCING SAFETY AND CONVENIENCE"**

CASE STUDY

MOVIEPASS

Ask a Different Question

Let's talk about Mitch Lowe; he's the guy that is credited with killing Blockbuster Video on every high street.

He did this by disrupting the market with RedBox, a company that asked different questions such as, "Why do I have to walk all the way to the high street to get my movie fix?" and "Why do I have to return it now or get fined, I paid to watch it right?" His model of posting out DVDs you could keep as long as you want ultimately catalysed the demise of the high street video store.

He then went on to found Netflix, a company that asked questions about how we consume TV and movies and led to many late-night binge fests of TV box sets, creating original content as it went.

Mitch is quite good at asking different questions and creating disruption.

I worry about MoviePass, his latest venture, though because in this case I think Mitch is asking the wrong questions.

So what is MoviePass? Well it's a subscription service that allows you to pay just $9.99 to join the MoviePass community and then you can go to the movies as much as you like for a month.

Yes. You heard right. Any movie, any chain of theatre, any ticket price, any amount of times, anywhere. All for $9.99.

$9.99 rarely gets you the price of admission to any showing, so essentially from the very first time you use it, MoviePass are losing and you are winning. How does that work? MoviePass send you a real Mastercard debit card, so that when you pick a movie and a viewing time, they credit your card with the exact amount required to buy that ticket. Real money.

Now to prevent you spending that money on Hubba Bubba Bubble Gum and Fidget Spinners, the company somehow lock the card so that it only becomes active in the proximity of the cinema and can only be spent on the ticket you selected. Nonetheless, if you wanted to spend thousands of dollars watching movies throughout the entire month for only $9.99 you could and MoviePass it appears will fund this at an unlimited potential loss to themselves.

But how is MoviePass funding this and what's their game? It's no con, they are losing money hand over fist in the belief that eventually their community will become so big that they will be able to force movie theatres into a revenue sharing arrangement. That may or may not happen eventually, but by this time MoviePass could easily be bust. Remember, every transaction they fund is lining the pockets of movie theatres in full price ticket sales, so I'm not sure that MoviePass is holding all the cards.

MoviePass says it will also make revenue from the data it collects from its target of 2.5 million subscribers, but that's a terribly expensive way to acquire customer data. There are additional problems here though, as on first use the app demands access to all your files, photos, contacts, location etc. on your phone. If you decline to hand over unfettered access to your phone, it locks you out and becomes unusable even if you've already paid for the service.

The company also seems to be struggling to meet the demand for this 'money-for-nothing' service as well. As user numbers grow by a rate of 150,000 every fortnight, there is now a backlog on sending out the cards.

Subscribers are advised to turn up at the cinema anyway and simply use their app, but despite payment appearing to be present on the phone, they are declined entry at the theatre having made the journey there. Over half of users have given the MoviePass app the lowest possible rank on Google's Play Store.

Some of the quotes from users are as follows: "App still doesn't work. I have had my card for a year. All they are doing is collecting fees." "Went to box office to get ticket, but they said my card wasn't accepted when they swiped it. Went to kiosk to try on my own with same result, 'try another card'."

It's important to note that Mitch Lowe has been disruptive in the past, where he has asked different questions and understood real needs. My question here is, "who really needs to watch films endlessly for an arbitrary cost of $9.99?" That's not an insight, nor is it apparently a business and I for one would not want to be bankrolling this experiment.

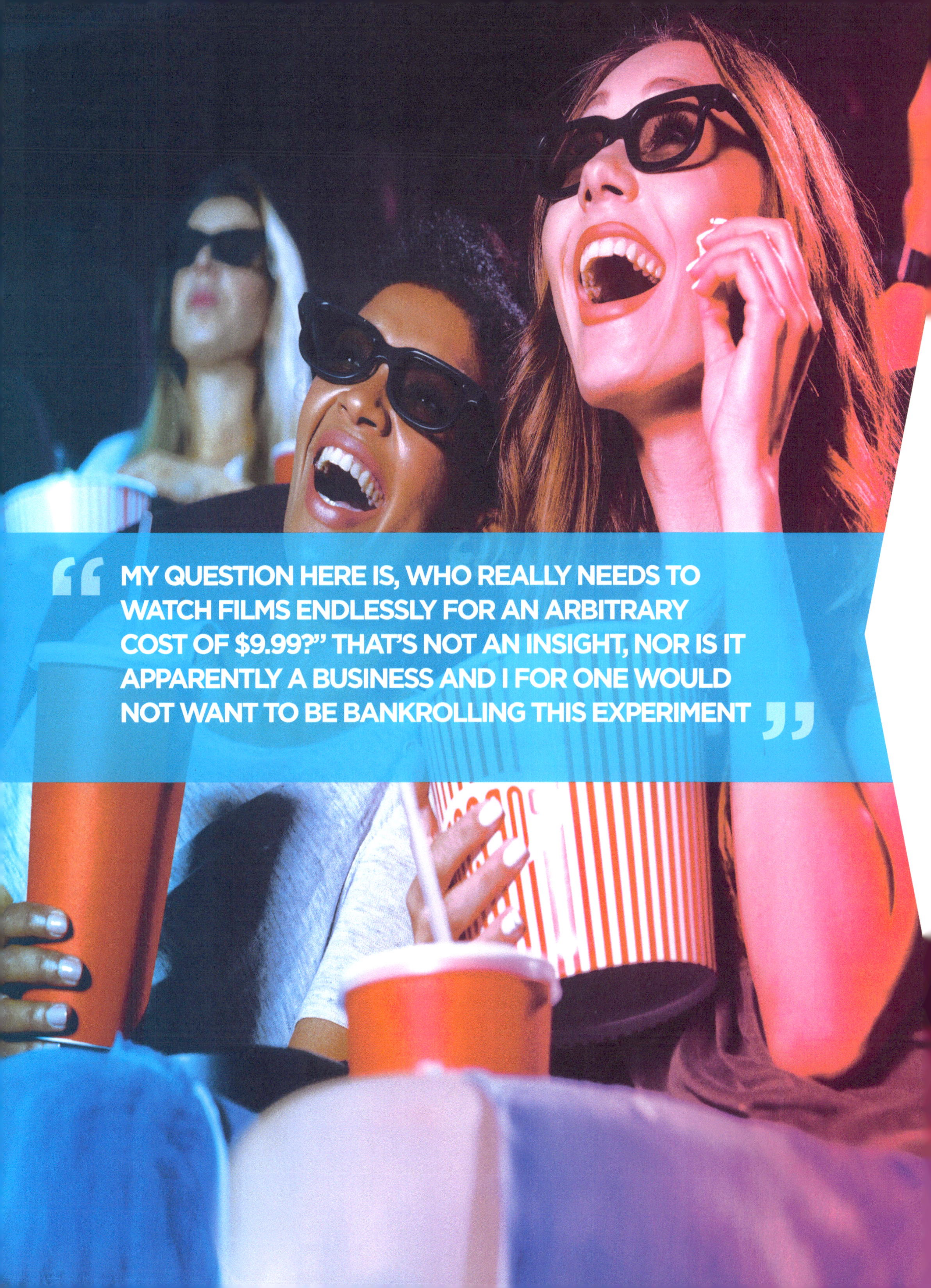

> "MY QUESTION HERE IS, WHO REALLY NEEDS TO WATCH FILMS ENDLESSLY FOR AN ARBITRARY COST OF $9.99?" THAT'S NOT AN INSIGHT, NOR IS IT APPARENTLY A BUSINESS AND I FOR ONE WOULD NOT WANT TO BE BANKROLLING THIS EXPERIMENT"

HABIT 3

THROW ONE BALL
Why it's your job to make choices, not your target's job...

There is a wonderful analogy used in advertising circles about the importance of single minded benefits and it goes like this. Imagine I stand in front of a room full of people, pick a willing volunteer and tell this target that I'm going to throw them a ball. Mentally they prepare to receive it, put their hands out in anticipation and as I throw, their eyes are glued to the moving ball as it loops gracefully through space until eventually they grasp it between their fingers and catch it. One ball thrown, one ball caught. Job done!

Now imagine a scenario where I have not one ball, but a bucket of balls, a great big selection of multi-coloured balls in a variety of sizes. I really should decide which ball to throw from the selection I have. But it's so hard to pick just one. Now doubt creeps in! What if I pick the wrong ball to throw? What ball would be most attractive to my target anyway? I never asked! Could be that they'd like more than one ball! At this point, what I call choice paralysis sets in.

So I throw all the balls! What choice did I have, I couldn't choose!

Before our volunteer in the audience knows what's happening, a huge rainbow coloured cloud of balls is rushing through space towards them. But here's the beauty of my decision (or lack of it!). Do I feel bad for having made no choice? Nope, I actually feel pretty damn good! And why? Because I post-rationalise my abject failure to throw a single ball as a positive. I presented choice to my target.

"Hey, now that guy gets to select the ball he likes himself," my inner voice assures me. "He didn't want me to limit him, he can make up his own mind from an abundance of options I have provided." My indecision and ineffectiveness as an innovator is instantly transformed into a virtue.

I stand back in confident anticipation that the audience member is going to watch the cloud of balls descend upon him, calmly select a ball of choice and gratefully catch it. The net result is that he catches the same amount of balls as if I'd just thrown one, except with the bonus of empowerment gifted benevolently from me to him.

In fact, he'll drop them all. Of course he will! There was an enormous bucket of balls chucked at him and his brain shut down with sensory overload. Very soon we'll all be stood in a confusing puddle of balls rolling round our feet.

Heavenly innovators know the most difficult part of their job is focusing down to a single-minded benefit. If we can't make that choice because it's difficult and painful to do, why would the target do our job instead? They won't; they have less skin in the game than we do, it's our job after all. They have better things to do than try and disentangle what the key benefit of our offer is and will quickly drop it and move on. They will favour the competitor's proposition that is clear and succinctly expressed, because the person selling it did the hard work rather than expecting them to. Simple Value Propositions with one single-minded benefit prevent over-engineered solutions and lead to elegant, easy to understand, ownable propositions.

When it comes to writing Value Propositions, this inability to select just one ball isn't a rare occurrence. In the thousands of Value Propositions I'm asked to critique each year it's probably one of the most frequent problems I see and it displays very serious underlying failings on the part of the innovator.

Heavenly innovators make a clear choice on their target (see Habit 1. 'Focus & Move the Mouse'), whereas their ill-disciplined counterparts try and target everyone. With a vague and disparate target, of course it becomes impossible to select the most significant benefit to offer.

Those that have good habits build their Value Propositions off the biggest unmet needs of their target customer, often referred to as insight driven innovation. In this approach, the single-minded benefit is easy to define, it's a commitment to solve the insight. Picking the most valuable ball to throw is simple once you know the target and their biggest unmet need. It's downright impossible if you don't!

Whilst those around them are throwing out multiple balls and creating what I call 'Swiss Army Knife Value Propositions' heavenly innovators know these hygiene factors are not the point of the exercise, they are not the benefit!

 Great innovators have laser sharp focus on a single-minded benefit to the exclusion of everything else that others would be tempted to include.

MOM INFLATABLE INCUBATOR

Throw One Ball

When people ask me where insights come from, they often envisage a focus group or elaborate piece of market research as the only source of insight. However the dictionary is very clear what defines an insight: "A discovery about something that was previously unknown, an 'AHA!' or "Eureka moment". It doesn't dictate anywhere where the source of that insight can come from.

James Roberts discovered the insight for MOM after watching a documentary on Syria where he learned that as a result of the stress of war infant mortality rates have soared, causing the country to lose nearly an entire generation to preventable infant deaths.

Of course there have been post-natal incubators available for years, they are invaluable pieces of equipment which help regulate the temperature of new born babies, keeping them warm.

Incubators also serve many other important functions too, as they provide insulation from noise, making it easier for infants to get plenty of rest. They keep the environment sterile, protecting babies from germs and lower the risk of infection. Because the incubator is fully enclosed it's possible to leave the infant in the device even when medical procedures are undertaken. This protects infants from too much handling.

James' insight however focused the target on babies that are not born in regular situations, where infrastructure such as roads, hospitals and even a reliable electrical supply can be relied upon. He realised that many babies are being born in environments that are harsher, more remote, less predictable and very often slap bang in the middle of a war zone.

He saw this as an opportunity to take these insights and develop a solution that would make a real difference.

The developer of the MOM Incubator was clear what he was solving. He didn't over-reach or try to resolve countless other issues, he had one clear insight and his solution throws just one ball.

James created a cheap, electronic, inflatable incubator designed with the single-minded purpose of reducing the number of premature child deaths in remote and ravaged parts of the world. As with Habit 1 – 'Focus and Move the Mouse', the designer narrowed his target to only areas of the world where established incubator would not be appropriate or effective.

According to the designer "The MOM Incubator offers a safe, medical grade environment for an infant to thrive in (equivalent to that a child would receive in a well-equipped Neonatal unit), whilst solving many of the problems of effectively incubating infants throughout the world."

The incredible thing about this Value Proposition is that it delivers the benefit at only 5% of the cost of a conventional incubator.

How does it deliver this medical grade environment for babies in such remote areas?

Well, the Reasons to Believe are clear.

Because the device is inflatable it can be compacted to a tiny amount of the size of a standard incubator with a 90% saving in weight.

By being battery powered it can be used in situ or charged and transported for use in areas where there is no electricity.

Also due to the fact that the MOM Incubator's inflatable body is so cheap, it's entirely disposable and can be completely replaced for every child. According to James: "This is not only cheaper than cleaning a system due to time costs, but it also could potentially alleviate the infection risk associated with incubators which is said to be the second largest killer of premature children after hypothermia."

On the company's website, they have a clear superiority statement, claiming that their solution is the only low cost solution that provides an environment similar to regular incubators, but that can be used in the most inhospitable locations.

This idea is simple, logical and single minded, so let's hope it is able to get to market. The company raised a seed round of £630,000 in June 2016. Currently, the company is approaching the clinical stage of development and plans to raise a £5 – 10 Million Series A by end of 2018.

"THE DESIGNER NARROWED HIS TARGET TO ONLY AREAS OF THE WORLD WHERE ESTABLISHED INCUBATORS WOULD NOT BE APPROPRIATE OR EFFECTIVE"

DYSON HAIRDRYER
Throw One Ball

Let me start by saying I'm a big fan of Dyson (pun intended). They are a British company that actually manufactures something and they invest heavily in design and development and employ hundreds if not thousands in trying to create innovative solutions.

So far so good. My issue is that very rapidly Dyson have evolved into a Technology Push organisation, that progressively throws multiple balls in order to justify the technology or IP they happen to own. As I've said earlier, if you don't know what problem you are solving you don't know what benefit to offer and you end up offering them all.

Dyson has its origins as a vacuum cleaner manufacturer and the thing that made it a leading brand which demanded a huge price premium was not just the clever miniaturisation of the cyclone technology, but the insight and single minded benefit of the Value Proposition that explained its value.

Dyson's insight for his vacuum cleaner was simple.

"All vacuum cleaners are becoming heavier and heavier, more and more powerful and using more and more electricity. But that's no use to you if they stop picking up dirt and dust when the bag gets full. In a perfect world, you need constant suction, so that your vacuum cleaner works just as well, all the time"

Straightforward, logical and focused. He threw a single ball and we all understood the benefit. "No bag, No loss of suction.." He looked for relevant insights and built a Value Proposition that solved it. A winning model.

Move on a few years. Dyson has now unveiled its first personal care product – the first hairdryer powered by a miniaturised air pump in the handle, using the same airflow technology as Dyson's desk fan.

Unfortunately with the launch of its new hairdryer Dyson seems to have lost the heavenly habit of throwing one ball. The mixed messages coming from Dyson about the benefit seem to deviate from, amongst other things, less damage to hair, lighter hairdryer, easier to handle, shorter time spent doing the task, better styling, less noise, lower energy consumption and less heat.

It's hardly single-minded or memorable! Yet its value needs to be crystal clear when Dyson are charging the earth for it! The £299 price tag makes it at least twice as expensive as other salon-grade dryers and 6 times more expensive than the most expensive consumer positioned 'professional' hairdryers on Amazon.

Like any manufacturer without the discipline of throwing one ball, they lazily leave working out what ball to catch to us. Most of us will drop everything and look elsewhere.

The company said it had invested £50m in the development of the device. I'd argue that the start point was neither targeted nor customer driven or else they'd know what ball to throw!

It would be naive to believe that they spent £50 million thinking about you and your hair drying needs. I do believe however that they spent a large amount in the development of a miniature version of their fan and then thought, "Where can we stick this?" This is not a subtle differentiation in approach. It changes everything!

The fact that most people are going to drop the balls he throws doesn't seem to worry James Dyson, drawing on a quote he gave at launch.

"I don't mind if I only sell 100 a year, as long as those 100 people think it's really good. I wouldn't make much money but that's not always the point. That's not what drives us, that's not what makes it exciting."

People seeing the relevance and need is not the point? It's not what drives us?

Appropriate pricing tied to a clear Value Proposition creates shareholder return. The intellectual challenge of creating clever things for the sake of it leads to disaster.

The final defining phrase in the Dyson communication tagline shows how the company is thinking;

"Dyson Supersonic, The Hairdryer we thought" - We thought?

The first comment beneath their launch advertising on YouTube says it all about the consumer response.

"The Hairdryer you thought what????"

"APPROPRIATE PRICING TIED TO A CLEAR VALUE PROPOSITION CREATES SHAREHOLDER RETURN. THE INTELLECTUAL CHALLENGE OF CREATING CLEVER THINGS FOR THE SAKE OF IT LEADS TO DISASTER"

HABIT 4

HAPPY TO HEAR NO!
Why it's better to know when stuff is destined to fail

I once facilitated market research for a client in a viewing facility in central London. The plan was to test the Value Proposition behind a new medical device and we had 6 healthcare professionals in the room who were recruited as experts in their field.

"Do you recognise this insight?" I began. "No," they responded without exception. "I don't have that problem and even if I did, I could solve that really easily in a multitude of ways already."

My job is to ensure that every angle is covered, so I kept approaching the need in as many ways as I could, looking for scenarios where the problem might be more pronounced or urgent. To no avail. "Sounds like you are trying to contrive a problem where none exists," pronounced one of the respondents. "Let's save you time, if I had 100 problems in my hospital that one would be priority 101!"

Got it! I went to the little viewing area behind the 2-way mirror to confer with my clients who were watching proceedings. "I think that's pretty definitive," I said, "There's no need."

"Please go back in and show them the finished device," came the response. "We've brought a working one with us."

It's probably worth taking time to consider the reality of most market research at this point. Nearly all insight research I have ever seen is a retro-active test run after the solution is already well progressed. Its intention is not really to hear whether a need is real or not, it's designed to justify what the team and business intend to do regardless.

"Can I just check what you intend to achieve by showing a finished solution given they've already said they don't have that problem?" I enquired. Then came the killer response:.."Well, perhaps if they see the finished solution they'll change their minds!"

Ah. This is the logic that says that presenting a shiny working technology with touch screen and flashing lights will override the fact that the insight doesn't exist.

So it was that I went back in front of the mirror and revealed the finished device to the healthcare professionals.

Now I'll admit that they did respond differently when they saw the finished device in all its glory. "Oh my god! You've already made it!" they said. The look on their faces told the story. "We thought you actually cared what we needed, but we can now see that you were going to do it regardless". "Oops, how embarrassing, we just said it was pointless" so "Let's see how we might dig you out of that hole you're in!"

Now even in this scenario the respondents couldn't quite bring themselves to say they needed it, but did make comments such as "I think someone may need that", or "if the light was right, Venus was in ascendency and you squinted at it just right, I think there might be a need."

Rest assured that following the research my clients wrote a PowerPoint to their senior management that said, "The customer interviews were very helpful and despite a few initial questions, the idea was well received overall. Let's continue all steam ahead!"

It's the same false logic that saw another client ask a customer recently, "Do you see the value of this idea?"; when the customer said no, the immediate response was, "Thank you, and should it be bigger or smaller?"

Too often teams are using research to justify the project. They believe their role is to circumnavigate all customer negatives to ensure the project comes to market anyway.

Senior management have a large responsibility here too. How often I see a project named after the technology such as 'internet connected lighting' rather than the need it addresses.

If a technology is so fixed in stone that the team is named after it, people's job titles contain the solution and it's on everyone's business card, then of course the technology will be protected at all costs.

Great innovators bring insight testing to the earliest opportunity in the development cycle. They don't waste resources building it or making shiny all singing, all dancing prototypes until the fundamental opportunity is validated.

If they hear that there is no opportunity, it's not an earth-shattering disaster as less money has been invested at that point and resources can be re-allocated to opportunities where solving them has more value.

Great innovators use market research ahead of spending too much time and resources to avoid costly mistakes rather than circumnavigating customer objections.

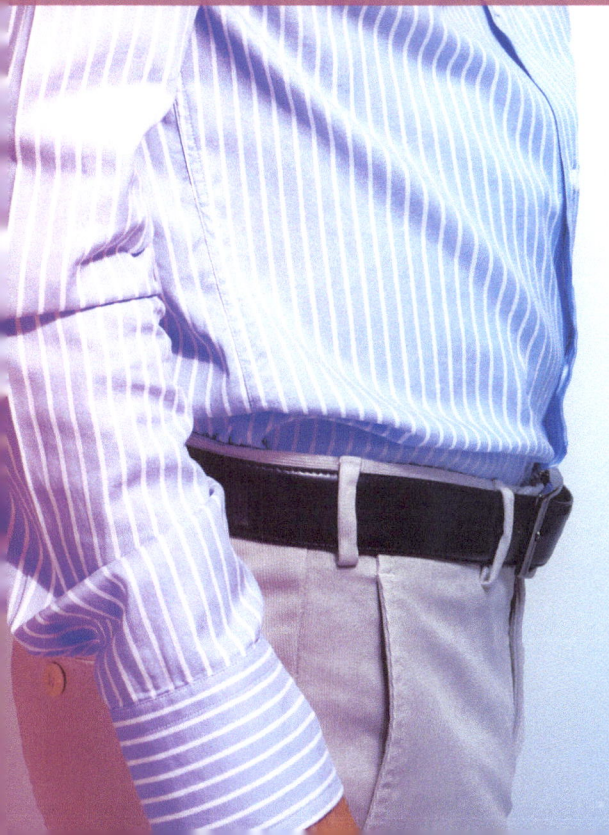
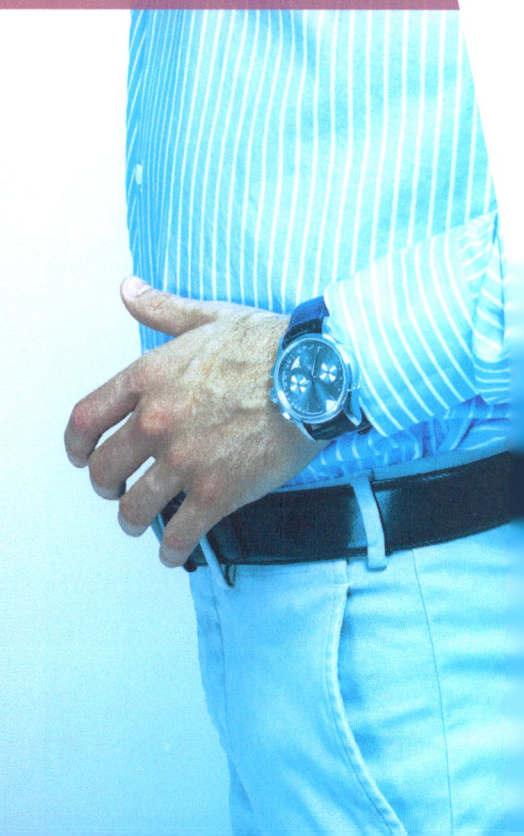

> "TOO OFTEN TEAMS ARE USING RESEARCH TO JUSTIFY THE PROJECT. THEY BELIEVE THEIR ROLE IS TO CIRCUMNAVIGATE ALL CUSTOMER NEGATIVES TO ENSURE THE PROJECT COMES TO MARKET ANYWAY"

FAIL FAST, FAIL EARLY, FAIL OFTEN

Happy to Hear No!

As you might imagine, it's difficult for me to point to a product that you have not heard of and that didn't come to market because behind the scenes the developers killed it.

A successful failure is somewhat of an oxymoron.

However, there are plenty of examples of products and services that initially failed and that eventually went on to be a success because the creators learned from the feedback, accepted change was necessary and developed something better.

James Dyson famously claimed to have created 5,127 prototypes of his bag-less vacuum cleaner before he got it right (perhaps he needs to revisit the Value Proposition and price of his hairdryer a few more times?).

Below I've compiled a shortlist of the greatest innovations that initially heard "No!" but built upon that rejection.

Apple Newton

Apple launched the Newton in 1993. It was supposed to be the first hand-held device that would replace a notepad and diary and would theoretically recognise your handwriting. Except the handwriting benefit, the focus of the Value Proposition was rushed and simply didn't work, meaning the product became the butt of a million jokes.

One cartoon strip in a daily US newspaper focused on the ineptitude of the Apple Newton as a running gag for a whole week!

When Steve Jobs arrived back at Apple he took great delight in killing the Newton at the first available opportunity as he felt it a product unworthy of Apple.

However, the failure of the Apple Newton and Steve Jobs' willingness to hear "No!" and put it out of its misery had long lasting positive consequences. Firstly the ARM processor that Apple had needed to develop to make the Newton work and support longer battery life went on to power millions of future devices.

The Newton didn't really die, it was improved, evolved and eventually became your smartphone and Apple made more money from these than anyone on earth.

Sales data suggests that by 2016, Apple had sold 1 billion iPhones worldwide.

The stylus and handwriting recognition didn't disappear either, they evolved into the Apple Pencil on your shiny new iPad Pro.

Overall the idea of a smart portable assistant that understands natural language led the way for Siri, Google Home, Alexa and Bixby.

The Apple Newton clearly wasn't the right solution, but it helped frame what the right solution should be.

Bubble Wrap

The designers who created bubble wrap in 1960 had actually tried to launch a new textured wallpaper. The product was not quite as fashionable or aesthetically pleasing to consumers as they had anticipated and the product failed. Not to be put off by hearing no, they began to investigate whether their technology would serve a purpose in the role of household insulation, but they again heard a resounding "No!". Finally, they repositioned the product with a Value Proposition for protecting delicate items during transit. It was used by IBM to package a newly launched computer and rapidly became a success.

WebOS

WebOS was supposed to be the future of mobile phone operating systems. It was developed and launched originally by Palm in 2009 and then acquired by HP in 2010. As part of a new strategy to create handheld devices HP decided to launch the TouchPad in 2011, a large tablet computer that ran WebOS as its flagship operating system.

The CEO of HP realised however that the TouchPad it had created was simply not good enough to compete with the likes of Apple and Android, and to the sound of much hand-wringing pulled the TouchPad from sale even before its official launch. The supply of TouchPads were unceremoniously sold off in a fire sale below cost at just $99 to the delight of savvy eBay shoppers.

In December 2011, however, HP announced that it would release WebOS as an open source license agreement and in 2013 LG acquired the rights.

If you have bought a fancy new LG TV in the last few years, then your TV is being run on WebOS, the failed operating system from the TouchPad fire sale.

Widely regarded as the best and most intuitive TV operating system, the failure of earlier innovations did not lead to the demise of WebOS, but the evolution and improvement.

"THERE ARE PLENTY OF EXAMPLES OF PRODUCTS AND SERVICES THAT INITIALLY FAILED AND THAT EVENTUALLY WENT ON TO BE A SUCCESS BECAUSE THE CREATORS LEARNED FROM THE FEEDBACK, ACCEPTED CHANGE WAS NECESSARY AND DEVELOPED SOMETHING BETTER"

TIDAL MUSIC STREAMING
Happy to Hear No!

A few years ago I was running a focus group with millennials about music and their listening habits. They were more than happy to download music digitally without ever physically owning the album. When I questioned them about what they were paying for, and what they actually owned as a result, it was all about convenience.

Ironically they were laughing at me for wanting to own a physical CD or DVD. "What are you going to do with that?" they asked. "Put it on a shelf and build a collection", I replied. "What a waste of space," seemed to be the response. To them, the ownership of media in a physical sense seemed to be an inconvenient anachronism. "I could rip it to MP3 and listen to it elsewhere," I said. "Or you could stream it and save the hassle completely," came the reply.

I saw there and then that the writing was on the wall for physical stores like HMV, Virgin Megastore and anyone else that didn't listen to these insights.

The inevitable result has occurred and when it comes to listening to music, the old-fashioned method of buying physical media such as CDs is in terminal decline. In 2002, CDs accounted for 96% of all music sales; by last year that number was down to less than 16%. There may be a nostalgic bounce for vinyl at the moment (mostly by old people like me who think the artwork on the sleeve is a key part of the proposition), but the signs are that this format isn't going to overturn the inevitable advance of digital music anytime soon.

What's interesting is that album sales are also declining, even digital albums, and that all the growth is coming from music streaming where paid subscriptions were worth 2.3 billion dollars in the US last year alone.

People clearly want to be able to select the tracks they want rather than the whole album, and to listen to them wherever they choose, be it on the phone, in the car or over their home hifi. They no longer care so much about actually owning the album itself.

They also don't care so much about the quality of the music recording either. Digital recordings listened to on a bike while peddling through the streets of Amsterdam, sat drinking cider in the park or streamed to a Ford Fiesta on the M6 motorway is of secondary consideration to convenience and omnipresent access.

Therefore the decision to launch Tidal in 2014 by Jay-Z and a collection of 12 highly paid music superstars seems to be fraught with issues.

What is Tidal and what makes its Value Proposition different?

Well firstly, Tidal claims to pay the highest percentage of royalties to music artists and songwriters within the music streaming market.

OK, let's stop there a moment. This isn't a situation like Fairtrade coffee, where the producers of the product were being oppressed and poorly remunerated for the time and resources they spent making the product. No one is crying into their Skinny Chai Latte over the exploitation of Jay-Z who is reported to have earned $650 million from his work, or Rihanna whose net worth is estimated at $250 million.

Tidal is a solution which benefits its ultra-rich owners more than anyone.

Then there is the strange decision to innovate on the technology and the quality of the music being streamed. Tidal offers two levels of digital music streaming service: Tidal Premium (high definition) and Tidal HiFi (lossless CD quality – FLAC-based 16-Bit/44.1 kHz – and MQA).

This is obviously essential when listening to music through earbuds on my phone in a Doncaster McDonald's.

The high-fidelity streaming simply slows down song loading times and offers negligible real-world sound difference at a hugely inflated price.

The universal consensus at launch was that this was a mistake and that Tidal needed to hear "No!", change the proposition or risk failure. But these are pop stars with egos that don't regularly listen to people telling them no.

And how is this all doing?

Tidal lost $28 million dollars in 2015, its growth is stalling with comparatively tiny numbers of paying users compared to competitors such as Spotify that have upwards of 50 million users and growing rapidly.

Worst of all, when Jay-Z appeared in court in October to testify in a sampling case, he forgot he owned Tidal when listing his businesses. "Yeah, yeah," Jay-Z said. "Forgot about that."

Not an inspiring response if you've invested in the company!

> "NO ONE IS CRYING INTO THEIR SKINNY CHAI LATTE OVER THE EXPLOITATION OF JAY-Z WHO IS REPORTED TO HAVE EARNED $650 MILLION FROM HIS WORK, OR RIHANNA WHOSE NET WORTH IS ESTIMATED AT $250 MILLION"

HABIT 5

HIDE THE HERO

Why your customer should take credit for what you've done

For decades now, BMW have communicated their Value Proposition through the tagline 'The Ultimate Driving Machine'.

That could just as easily be expressed as 'The Ultimate Machine', right? In fact it would take less words to say and it roughly approximates to the same thing doesn't it? No! That one little word 'driving' changes everything. It says that the insight behind buying and owning a BMW is the driving experience, the hero of the piece is consequently the driver and the machine is simply the ultimate enabler.

When a BMW goes around a corner at 100mph, the car has a sophisticated panoply of technologies working behind the scenes including traction control, limited slip differential and more. Is it helpful therefore to tell the driver that the car is essentially driving and that they might as well not be there? That if the car takes the bend successfully that it was the car, not the driver, who was the hero? Not given the attitudinal segmentation of a BMW driver who revels in the 'Joy' of driving. To even infer that they weren't really driving would be the equivalent of consumer insight Hari Kari for BMW.

Now don't get me wrong, if the car were to skid on that corner, flip upside down a few times and land in a field on its roof, that would be bad too! BMW's technology would have failed the driver and made them look like a bad driver. Perhaps the driver really needs all that assistance to pull off the manoeuvre and BMW is enabling the driver to have the ultimate driving experience, the key here is that there is a significant difference between seeing the technology you create as a tool for the user rather than insisting that the user acknowledges your solution as the hero and by default themselves as less qualified, less engaged and less effective?

Based on many years of working with technology companies, this reality that the customer is the hero simply isn't the natural start point for communication.

If for one second the customer might dare take credit for delivering the benefit of a product by being a skilled surgeon, a great driver or a talented designer, then the manufacturer feels compelled to step in and snatch back credit.

"Oh, don't think you did that!" they scream through their advertising. "We did that, not you!", "Have you any idea how many years of R&D went into making that a reality?", "You're actually irrelevant.".

One wonders why companies feel the need to swap the positive emotions of satisfaction and empowerment for the slightly less attractive ones of obsolescence and irrelevance?

Perhaps technology companies believe that unless they constantly point out how clever the technology is behind the scenes, no one will buy their product, like a paranoid inversion of the Wizard of Oz who keeps pulling back his own curtain to show how the trick is performed.

A few years ago I was with a team who were interviewing radiologists about a new piece of software that used pattern recognition algorithms to identify and classify tumours in images. "We do that already and pretty effectively," stated one of the radiologists. "Well then this will make you obsolete," came the reply from the development team!

Nice segue into the next part of the conversation, "Would you like to buy one?" I thought at the time. However, before they could ask this, the radiologist provided the following withering put-down.

"My understanding is that a passenger plane can take off, fly and land without actually needing any human involvement," he said. "Yet every time I board a plane there's a pilot standing in the doorway reassuring me that the computer has a skilled person at its controls. When you're happy to send a family member to be diagnosed and sent for surgery without someone like me involved, then I'll be obsolete, but until that time, let's assume I'm still pretty important!"

The role of technology is to enable the user to achieve things they otherwise couldn't, and the role of marketing is to allow to them think they did that themselves! As Maslow very clearly pointed out in his hierarchy of needs, customers and consumers pay a lot more for how things make them feel rather than how they rationally achieve that.

Great technology brands 'take one' for the team so that the customer or user stays in the limelight.

 Great innovators are comfortable letting their target customer take the credit for the success of the solution rather than insisting that the technology and method is acknowledged as the hero.

"THE ROLE OF TECHNOLOGY IS TO ENABLE THE USER TO ACHIEVE THINGS THEY OTHERWISE COULDN'T, AND THE ROLE OF MARKETING IS TO MAKE THEM THINK THEY ACHIEVED THAT THEMSELVES!"

PATEK PHILIPPE

Hide The Hero

I have small pores in my armpits. When it's warm the sweat that comes out of them heats up as my arms stay close to my body and the bacteria contained within starts to breed. Over time these bacteria begin to form a nasty smell known as body odour making me less attractive to those I'm standing next to on the Tube!

With me so far?

Well I can fix that by squirting something on my pits that blocks the sweat from emerging, we'll call that an antiperspirant. I could also spray a stronger smell on to my sweaty armpits that doesn't eradicate the issue but at least masks it. We'll call that a deodorant.

What I've just described is true, however the overly functional way I communicated it demeans its attractiveness (I hope you weren't nodding along thinking that all sounded attractive!).

As mentioned elsewhere in this book Maslov's hierarchy of needs explains how describing the emotional reward will always create more value than the function.

Whilst rationally the idea of a deodorant is worth $1, the promise of being sexually, voraciously attractive to women for the next 24 hours so I'm beating them off with a stick (the Axe effect) is miraculously worth 200% more. It's still the same thing, but I've simply hidden the technology and made the user the hero. It's no longer a smell that masks my own body odour, it's Gravity or Africa!

I'm a sex god, rather than Unilever is a great manufacturer of deodorants. My favourite exponent of the Hide the Hero habit is Patek Philippe, the Swiss watch manufacturer founded in 1839.

Let's step back and think about Swiss watches for a moment and what makes them unique. They all have an association with quality, expertise in time piece manufacturing, heritage and tradition, quality components. All of them.

The problem is that rationally this value proposition would be equally true for Rolex, Breitling, Tissot, TAG Heuer. All Swiss watches are pretty reliable.

If I'm Patek Philippe I want to be able to communicate my Value Proposition, but make these rational commonalities seem less important while making myself seem unique.

Of course I could try and optimise the technology, make the size or number of the cogs the hero or the exact composition of the alloys the hero. I could perhaps try and get the target to focus on exact specifications such as the average lifetime of a watch, or the tiny number of quality control issues.

The problem is my watch may last 75 years and a Rolex could last roughly the same. The function and technology is hard to differentiate without getting into a tit for tat specification game with competition.

Worst still, someone could point out that the average Casio watch also lasts around 75 years and the whole house of cards comes crashing down.

So Patek Philippe have built their Value Proposition in a different way: they have avoided the function and focused on the emotion. They have chosen to sacrifice communicating the inner workings of their watch on the altar of making the target owner the hero.

Patek Philippe's positioning is "You never really own a Patek Philippe, you merely look after it for the next generation", their tagline is "Start your own tradition".

The communication of the Value Proposition is clear.

If you buy a Patek Philippe watch, you can hand it on to your son or daughter and have the emotional reward that every time they look at that watch, they thinks of you and the memories you shared together. This positioning escalates Patek Philippe up Maslov's hierarchy of needs and stops them being compared rationally with the functionality of all other Swiss watches.

Clearly the watch needs to last a long time or that promise is meaningless, but exactly how long, how does it do that, how many cogs are in the watch? God only knows! Doesn't matter.

This is the reason that Patek Philippe broke world records in 2016 by selling their 1518 watch for $11 million in a Geneva Auction.

The Value Proposition of *Looking after a watch for the next generation* is the same as saying *This watch lasts a long time*. The first communication however is an elegant demonstration of Hiding the Hero and maximising the value of the solution as a result, the second is communicating the watch as the hero and is the equivalent of a sweaty armpit Value Proposition!

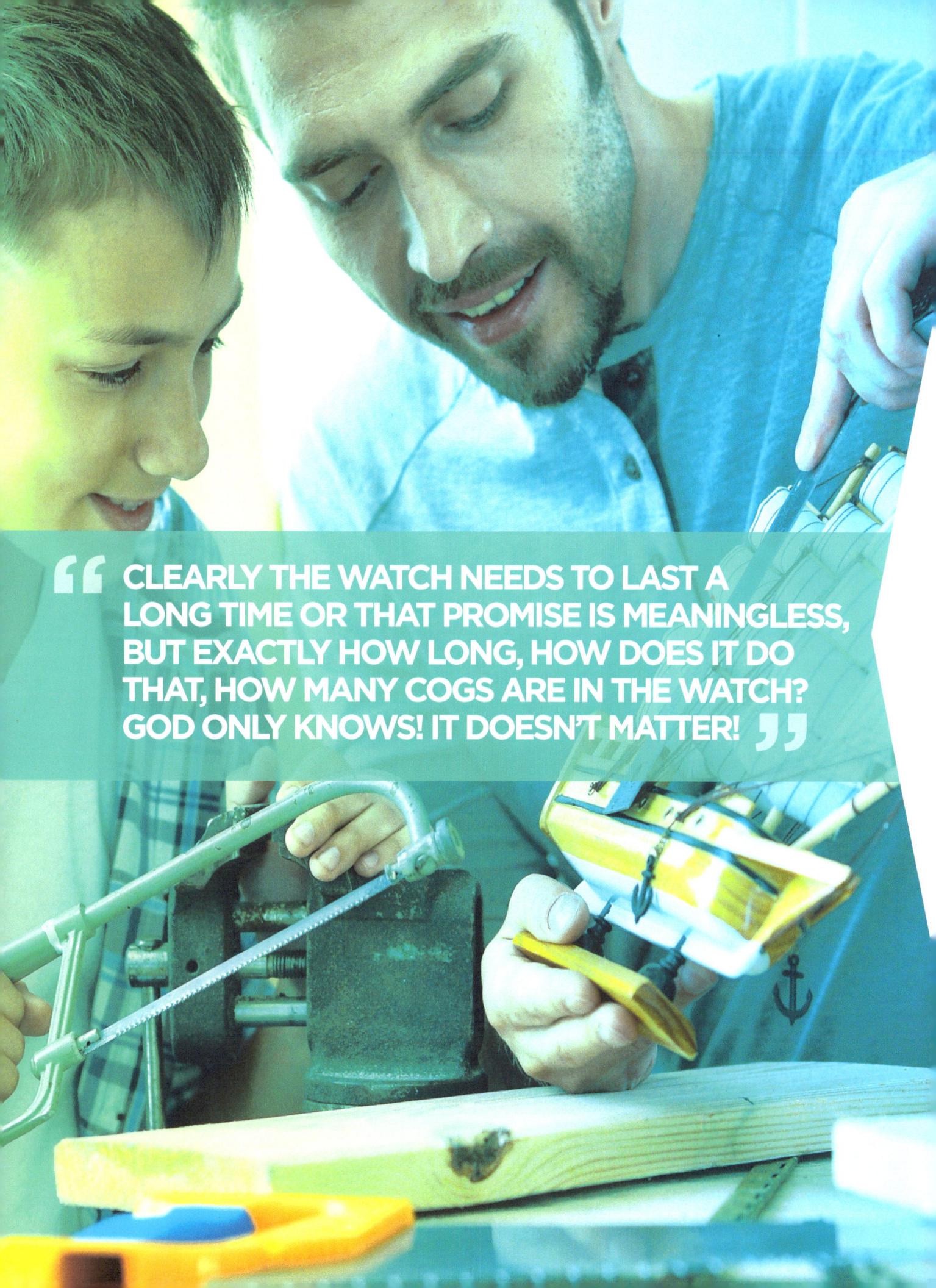

> "CLEARLY THE WATCH NEEDS TO LAST A LONG TIME OR THAT PROMISE IS MEANINGLESS, BUT EXACTLY HOW LONG, HOW DOES IT DO THAT, HOW MANY COGS ARE IN THE WATCH? GOD ONLY KNOWS! IT DOESN'T MATTER!"

NIKE HYPERADAPT 2.0

Hide the hero

I always teach on my training courses that Value Propositions do not exist in a vacuum.

At the top of a strategic cascade is your company or brand Value Proposition and then below that is a descending series of tiers of other Value Propositions (Business Group, Region, Product Line, Product etc.).

A product should never launch without ensuring that the target, insight and benefit are clearly aligned with what the rest of the organisation is doing and communicating.

Strategy never cascades upwards, it cascades top-down. As a product manager, I don't have free reign to choose my strategy, it can only be a subset of the decisions made at the levels above. Anything else would lead to anarchy.

If I do innovate something non-strategic it has two clear disadvantages, firstly you are swimming against the tide and receive no halo advantage from the company's other marketing activities, and secondly you seriously risk undermining the brand positioning and the credibility of other products within the portfolio.

Presumably Nike has a strategy that cascades top-down in this way?

So what is the overall Value Proposition of Nike?

Well Nike's positioning is 'Just Do It', a tagline that encapsulates the insight that every human being is potentially an athlete.

Cascading down from this, it sells premium sports equipment which includes a multi-million running shoe business aligned to this higher-level Nike Value Proposition.

Its products have become a symbol of status, and everything that Nike sets out to do is focused on engendering the emotional response that the target user "will gain a sense of achievement that they can do anything".

Let's skip to my 6-year-old for a moment. He doesn't want to learn to tie his laces.

I think he's happy that his Spiderman shoes have pretend laces and that, secretly, he can slip them on without applying much effort, but he'd like the world to think he can actually do up his laces like a big boy can.

I often try and encourage him into learning to tie his laces with the inferred threat that he wouldn't want people to think he needs someone to do them for him. He responds well to that, after all, who wants others to know you can't even do up your own laces?

Back to the Nike target. Remember them? The athlete who can do anything.

Meet Nike's HyperAdapt 2.0 running shoes, monumentally over-engineered and exorbitantly priced at $720 dollars: a pair of running shoes that tie your laces for you. Not secretly, but conspicuously!

Yes you heard right.

If Nike wanted to save its customers a little time and effort, it could have made some slip-on trainers like those Spiderman provides for my 6 year old. They could have created Velcro fasteners at a fraction of the cost. But no, they create $720 running shoes that automatically lace themselves and scream to the world you'll pay through the nose for that, because doing it yourself is a bit tricky.

How do they work? The laces tighten when your foot hits the heel sensor and then just in case those around you missed the fact that you can't tie your own laces, lights start flashing during the auto-activated lace-tightening procedure. All that's missing is a trumpet emerging from the heel to produce a choral fanfare announcing what a complete tool you are.

You haven't heard the best bit yet!

Your shoes run on electricity and won't work unless you charge them! You heard me right! You can't wear your shoes without charging the battery first?! Hardly the best encapsulation of 'Just Do It!'

I have a policy in my house of not letting those unable to tie their own shoe laces go anywhere near the plug sockets!

I find myself picturing the following scene:

"How did you do in the marathon at the weekend, Dave?"

"I'm afraid I couldn't compete at the last minute."

"Were you injured?"

"No, unfortunately I couldn't find a plug socket at the start line so my shoe laces wouldn't tie!"

You couldn't make this stuff up!

> "THE LACES TIGHTEN WHEN YOUR FOOT HITS THE HEEL SENSOR AND THEN JUST IN CASE THOSE AROUND YOU MISSED THE FACT THAT YOU CAN'T TIE YOUR OWN LACES, LIGHTS START FLASHING DURING THE AUTO-ACTIVATED LACE-TIGHTENING PROCEDURE"

HABIT 6

BOUNCE JUST ONCE

Why your user shouldn't need to change for your technology to become relevant.

In my training I use a real life example of a dish soap manufacturer in Brazil who found that the consumers in the country thought that dish soap was disproportionately too expensive. Not just their brand, but all brands.

It was fascinating that consumers in adjacent Latin American countries did not share that view. I use this case study to explore how project managers, marketers and engineers would go about solving this brand's dichotomy.

To help set context, I divulge choice information about Brazilian consumers' behaviour in the kitchen: I explain that they do not put the plug in the drain unlike many other countries. Instead of washing multiple dishes in a sink full of soapy water, Brazilians squirt dish soap on their sponge and then wash one dish at a time. As the running water from the tap hits the sponge it washes the detergent out and down the drain requiring the user to re-apply a new dose of detergent for every dish they wash.

No wonder they think that dish soap is too expensive; they are using 20 times more than the rest of us.

Once placed in the shoes of the dish soap manufacturer it's amazing how consistently my trainees make a mental leap to solve the problem.

"OK", they say. "That problem is an easy fix! We just need to show the Brazilians that little rubber stopper hanging on the chain in the sink, and explain that it goes in the hole at the bottom!"

What?!

Are we really suggesting that Brazilians haven't spotted that hole? Or that funny looking rubber thing next to it, with exact hole shaped dimensions? "Perhaps they have noticed it," they concede, "but need us to educate them to use it, so that our dish soap becomes relevant."

And right there is the rub, the honest distillation of so much thinking that goes on in clever, high-tech, engineering driven companies every day. If the consumer does not behave or see the relevance of a product we are developing, then that's not our fault, it's the user's problem. And despite whatever solid rationale they may have for behaving in that way, we need to simply re-educate them to behave and think differently (what I call mental bounce 1) and then we are in a position to communicate our solution and sell them our Value Proposition (bounce 2).

The truth is, '2 bounce innovation' is a fantasy: wishful thinking designed to prevent innovators seeking to understand why users behave the way they do or having to develop solutions sympathetic to actual habits and beliefs. It's also financially suicidal.

Most of my clients' companies have a business model where engineering and R&D take the lion share of investment. This means that their above the line and below the line marketing spend is tiny in real terms. 2 bounce innovation requires a phenomenal investment up front to re-educate the customer to change ingrained practices and attitudes. Even the world's largest marketing companies struggle to pull off this trick with their multi-million dollar communication reserves.

You didn't need that start button on Windows, you know. You thought you did, but you didn't. It didn't really make sense to have a different layout on a computer than a phone or a tablet with a touch screen. You thought it did, but it didn't! Microsoft knew. They told you over and over that you should change the way you interacted with your computer so their new operating system in Windows 8 made sense.

Did you change your habit, despite the phenomenal amount of resources Microsoft through at you? No. So welcome back start button on Windows 10. A single bounce, rather than a 2 bounce innovation.

And why did those Brazilians behave the way they did when it came to washing dishes? Well, they thought that the spices and colours of their food transferred from dish to dish if they didn't. They'd been taught to collect a little cream from a dish on their fingers and clean each dish separately, and over the years that habit made sense when it came to squirting dish soap on their sponge too.

And how did the manufacturer resolve this in just one bounce? They created a liquid detergent that solidified on contact with water so Brazilians can continue to squirt it on their sponge, but it doesn't wash out.

No expensive re-education, no changing the habit of generations, just clever innovation and technology based around how people behave in real life.

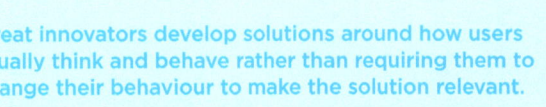

Great innovators develop solutions around how users actually think and behave rather than requiring them to change their behaviour to make the solution relevant.

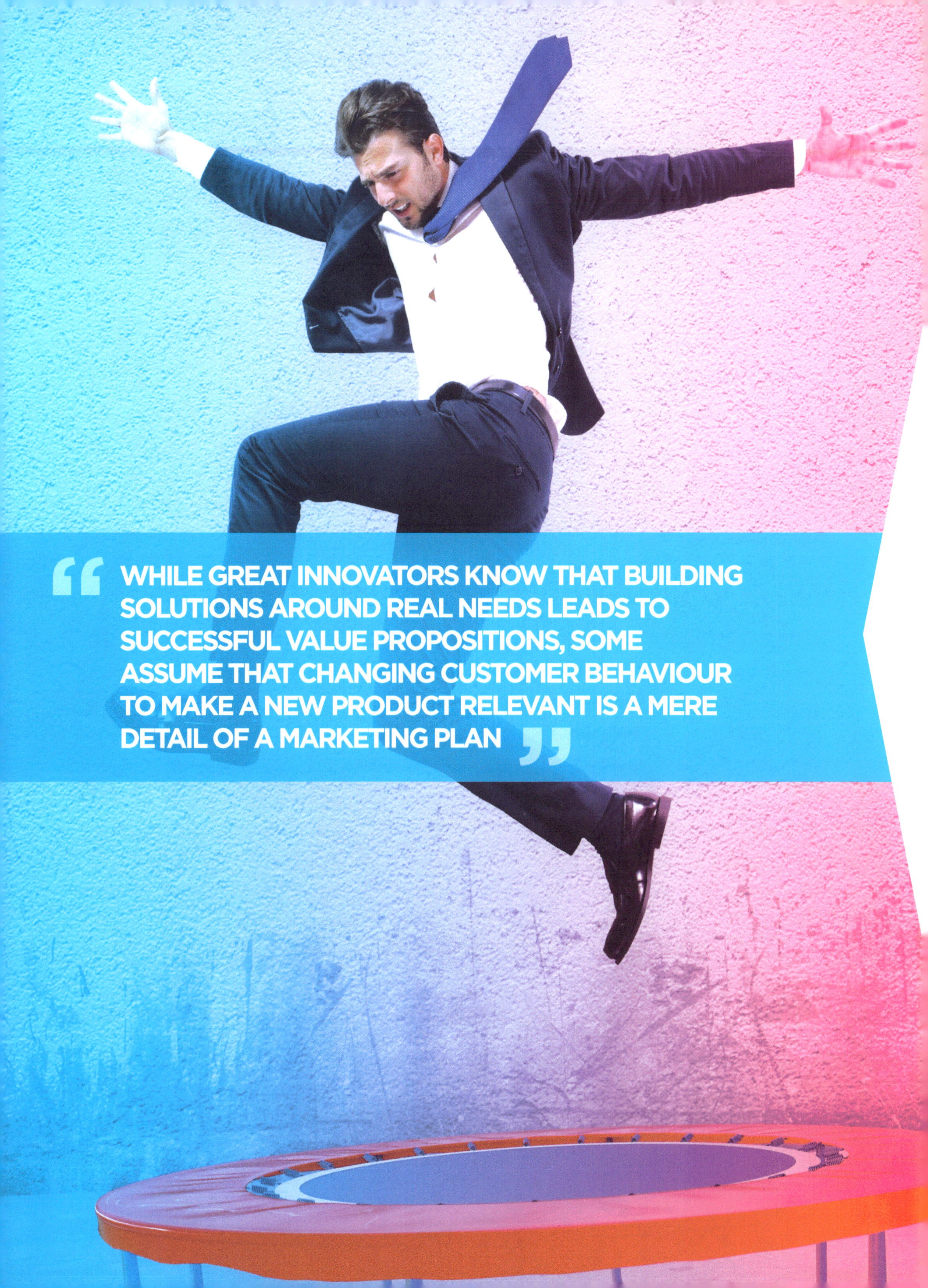

> **WHILE GREAT INNOVATORS KNOW THAT BUILDING SOLUTIONS AROUND REAL NEEDS LEADS TO SUCCESSFUL VALUE PROPOSITIONS, SOME ASSUME THAT CHANGING CUSTOMER BEHAVIOUR TO MAKE A NEW PRODUCT RELEVANT IS A MERE DETAIL OF A MARKETING PLAN**

SAMSUNG FLEXWASH & ADDWASH

Bounce Just Once

Having spent my early years in marketing working for the world's 2 largest detergent manufacturers, P&G and Unilever, I have first-hand experience of how consumer insights are used to create great innovation in the laundry category.

The insight that children get dirty and that is normal and healthy led Unilever to position Persil and OMO on the Value Proposition of 'Dirt is Good', one of the best and most disruptive campaigns in 50 years of detergent marketing. While the competition were trying to encourage us that dirt is bad (particularly blood, oil and egg apparently) and that we should change our habits and avoid it at all costs (2 bounces), Persil was telling us that getting dirty was fine and natural and we should carry on (1 bounce) confident that their product would resolve the issue anyway and get our clothes clean again.

However, whilst the positioning and format of the detergent you use may be changing and evolving constantly, from tablets to liquicaps to gels, the washing machine you put it in seems resolutely uninspired.

Samsung may have had a bad year when it comes to their Galaxy Note mobile phones creating impromptu firework displays in your pocket on transatlantic flights, but there's better news from their washing machine department.

Their new FlexWash washing machine seems to have brought genuine insight driven innovation to the category for the first time in years.

As I have explained in the Bounce Just Once habit, great innovation doesn't try and change consumer behaviour and habits, but seeks to build upon existing needs to create relevant disruption.

So what insights into existing behaviour did Samsung use when developing their washing machine?

According to Samsung, "research on U.S. consumer laundry habits, 87% of U.S. consumers surveyed sort their laundry into lights and darks, different fabric types, and degrees of dirtiness, while 70% of consumers surveyed run two or more back-to-back washes."

Essentially, we already separate out our clothes and wash them in different ways and the inflexibility of washing machines means we need to run the machine multiple times for these different loads.

Now we could create innovation that tries to persuade people not to do that, a solution that tries to change that habit. We could create a washing machine where all items go in together and we could tell people that the technology could cope and that there would be no consequence. This however would be 2 bounce innovation and would require huge shifts in belief and behaviour before the solution was ever adopted.

Samsung have gone for a more elegant 1 bounce solution.

The FlexWash washing machine has a main compartment with five cubic feet of capacity to handle normal or bulky loads. It also has the FlexWash top-loader which adds another cubic foot of capacity and is built to wash smaller loads or different coloured items separately from the main load.

The most important benefit is that both of these compartment can be set to wash your clothes simultaneously. Separated laundry is still washed all at once.

Inevitably the machine sports many side features and technologies which baffle and bamboozle with their complex acronyms and jargon: SuperSpeed™, Ecobubble, PowerFoam™, and Vibration Reduction Technology (VRT). However the single minded benefit of being able to separate and care for your clothes more efficiently shines through from their Value Proposition.

Personally, my biggest problem when it comes to washing clothes is that once I've loaded the washing machine, set the program, added the detergent and switched it on, I find a rogue child's sock on the stairs. Like Kamikaze cloth escapees, there will always be a pair of underpants that has leapt out of the laundry basket and hidden just long enough to allow the water to fill up in the machine and prevent me from stopping the cycle and adding it into my washing.

Those guys at Samsung have this insight covered too!

Their AddWash washing machine has a smaller door within the bigger door. The AddWash feature allows you to stop the machine, add items of laundry through the smaller door and let the washing carry on from where it left off. If you need to top up the detergent or fabric conditioner at that point you can!

Genius.

The definition of an insight according to the Oxford English dictionary is "an 'AHA!' moment"; your response to hearing it should be, "That's so obvious, why has no one ever done that before?". For me the FlexWash and AddWash innovations are the perfect encapsulation of that thinking and as such, I expect Samsung to go a long way in creating great disruptive innovation that sells.

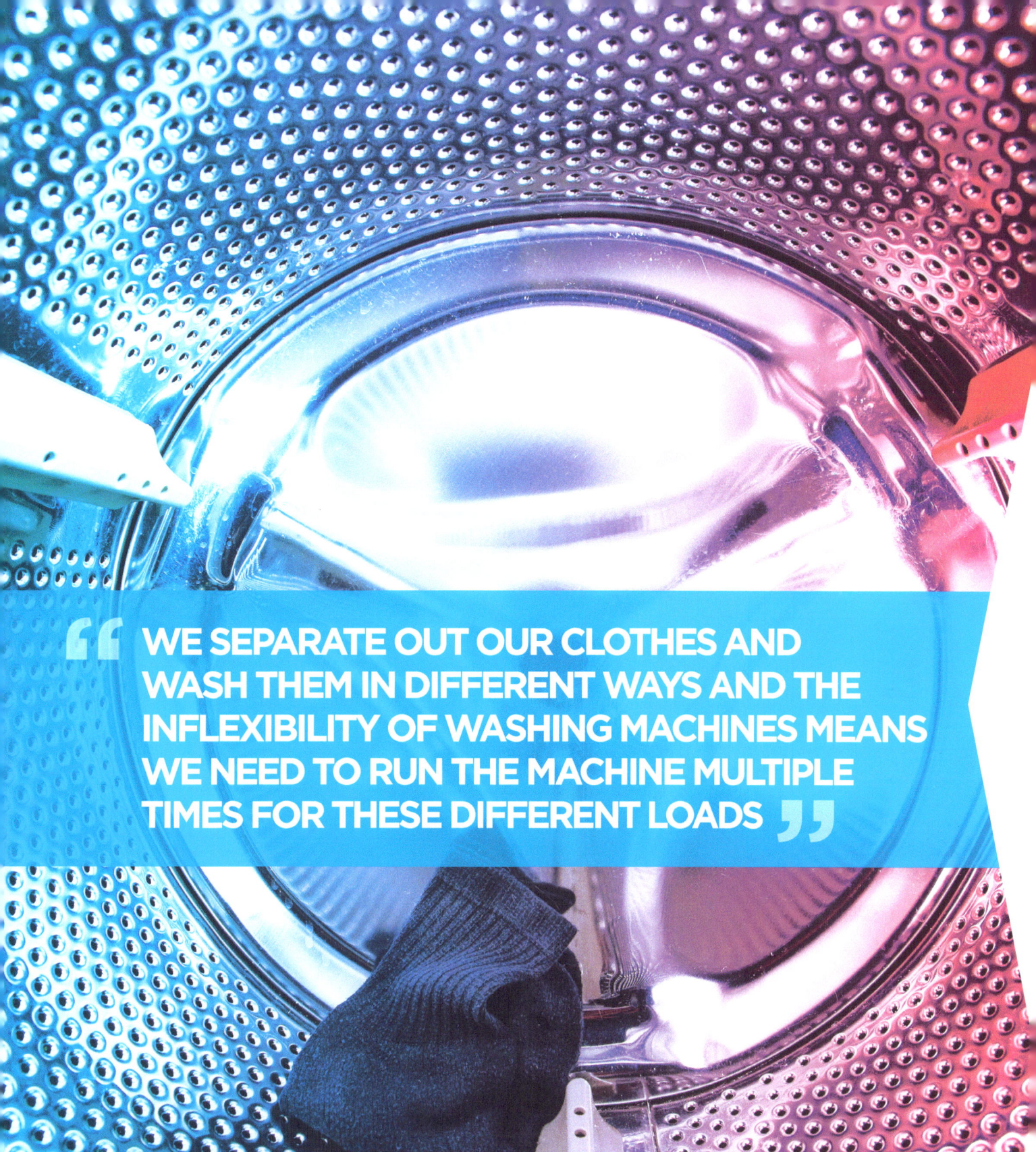

"WE SEPARATE OUT OUR CLOTHES AND WASH THEM IN DIFFERENT WAYS AND THE INFLEXIBILITY OF WASHING MACHINES MEANS WE NEED TO RUN THE MACHINE MULTIPLE TIMES FOR THESE DIFFERENT LOADS"

JUICERO

Bounce Just Once

For many years I've told the story during my insight training about the internet connected iron that I was asked to consult on.

It held the owner's phone number, email address and cell phone number and if they left their iron on at home, it called or messaged them a warning to get back in their car, drive home and turn the iron off.

The killer part of this story for me was that fact that the same team had another iron that contained an gyroscope and accelerometer. If you didn't pick the iron up, it turned itself off.

When I asked them why they selected to launch the internet connected iron vs the alternative, it was clear to them. People expect high-tech solutions from high-tech companies.

Somehow to have launched the solution that delivered clear benefits in a sensible way would have been failure because it wasn't technologically challenging.

So it was with a heavy heart that I heard about the Juicero story over the weekend.

If you haven't heard about this debacle, buckle up. It's a doozie.

Juicero has positioned itself as the next hardware/software combination to come out of Silicon Valley. A piece of expensive electronics with a new type of business model where the consumer pays through the nose for an ongoing consumable component.

Think Nespresso machine for fruit juice.

Of course it's all monumentally over engineered, promising a Wi-Fi connected juice-pressing gadget with customised packets of pre-prepared organic fresh fruit and vegetables squeezed into a glass by a machine that applies "8,000 pounds of pressure".

And because it's high-tech and because Silicon Valley seed fund managers seem to have more money than common sense, it's received $100 million dollars of funding for what turns out to be an unqualified and fruitless innovation (excuse the pun).

And the problem?

Well, according to the Times, "In a test, reporters from Bloomberg found that they could wring 7.5oz (210ml) of juice in a minute and a half from the recyclable bags. The machine, built of 'aircraft grade aluminium and precision-forged gearing components', took about two minutes to yield 8oz. Far from doing 'something truly monumental', Juicero appears to have been attempting to sell a $399 device for emptying packets of pre-juiced fruit and vegetables."

To add insult to injury, the company defends the machine by saying that it has clever technology on board which can read the best before date of the sachets and cross reference it against on online databases automatically.

Wow!

Or, of course, the consumer could read the date on the label just as easily without shelling out nearly $400. But why give the consumer credit for even being able to read a label despite that being their existing habit when you can demand new rituals and steps which require the user to bounce more than once?

I'm glad I'm not the venture capital guru that's got to explain those findings to my boss.

But have those masters of innovation in Silicon Valley shown any hubris or contrition at the revelation that their $100 million folly is worse than squeezing a bag by hand?

No, banish such a thought from your minds.

Jeff Dunn, Juicero's CEO, said: "You won't experience that value by hand-squeezing Produce Packs. What you will get with hand-squeezed packs is a mediocre experience."

The value I'll experience, Jeff, is more juice in my glass and the feeling of $399 more dollars in my pocket.

It never ceases to amaze me the blinkered belief that clouds judgement when it comes to technology companies.

You see people contesting on LinkedIn and other forums that the rules we all understand simply don't apply to them and the rest of us just don't get it.

We do get it! We can tell when something is pointless and over complicated! We can tell when a technology is trying to tell us that it can do something in a complicated way that the consumer could easily do better by hand.

Remember Jeff, when it comes to juicers, no one wants to be perceived as a sucker!

And the inevitable news broke in September 2017 that Juicero is shutting down. The company is suspending the sale of both its juice packets and its Juicero Press device blaming the difficulties of building a national supply chain (rather than accepting it was a crap idea). All employees have been given 60 days notice and the investors have lost all their money! Just another day in the world of the galactically stupid who think they know better than the rest of us.

> "BECAUSE IT'S HIGH TECH [...] JUICERO RECEIVED $100 MILLION DOLLARS OF FUNDING FOR WHAT TURNS OUT TO BE AN UNQUALIFIED AND FRUITLESS INNOVATION"

HABIT 7

LOOK DOWN THE CHAIN

Why you need to look beyond the purchaser for insight in B2B

The pushback I hear most frequently from a B2B team when I stand in front of them for the first time is: "Insight driven innovation doesn't work in B2B."

However, the truth is that just as there are immutable truths of physics and mathematics, there are also universal principles in marketing too!

What those developing insights in B2B need are tools and techniques that take into account the existence of a complex B2B stakeholder chain. That is not the same thing as changing the rules, just applying the rules appropriately to fit the context.

In B2B we can have many stakeholders flowing away from us down the chain to the end user; they all have different roles in the ultimate adoption and success of our solution from purchasing, to specifying, to installing, using and experiencing it. So far, nothing contentious, right?

Where many in B2B go wrong is with the myopic view that the only stakeholder's insight that really matters is the purchaser or payer! "As they are the ones with the cheque book, theirs is the only opinion that matters!"

The problem with that approach is, I have clients that position themselves as the experts in security, in food, in telecommunications. Their customers would legitimately anticipate that this means they have insights in the totality of the market and stakeholders rather than just into the one stakeholder who happens to hold the cheque book!

From this flawed piece of thinking, all problems emanate.

Just because I pay for something doesn't mean I understand what's needed, does it? Imagine I'm buying presents at Christmas for my 4 little boys. For the toys that will be delivered on Christmas Eve, they will almost certainly be the end user in the value chain. They tell me what they want (they make a list and check it twice!), what are the latest trends, the things they lose sleep at night wishing for, and I play the role of the payer (as usual).

Do I take into account their wishes when making my purchase decision, or do I dictate to them what they will get based on my own criteria? I could try the latter, but in my experience if it's not what they needed or wanted it will go unused and we all end up dissatisfied.

So why is it any different in a hospital, for example? Do we envisage that the purchasing department knows exactly what is going on in every aspect of the hospital? If I ask the purchasing department in a children's hospital to tell me what happens in the MRI suite would they know? Why would they hold deep insight on every nuance of the hospital's workings?

In this scenario the payer may be sitting in Cincinnati and there may be 150 hospitals in a chain all around the world. They may be buying everything from X-ray machines to the paint for the lines in the car park, but many innovators use just this payer's demands to determine the devices that an expert cardiologist will need to use in Shanghai. What nonsense.

In every meaningful innovation process the premise is the same: if you derive your insight from the person at the coal face (the person closest to the problem or most clued up about the need) you will create more relevant solutions.

Developing insights with users and consumers further down the chain and then using them to inform and enhance the business of your immediate customer isn't arrogant, it's called proactivity.

Those that approach insight generation in this manner find that insight brought to the attention of the payer has the potential to shift their paradigm; those that focus entirely on the payer's insight tend to hear the same old request, "I want the same solution as last year except cheaper.".

 **Great innovators don't focus exclusively on the purchaser's needs, but leverage the needs of other stakeholders to shift the paradigm of the decision makers.**

"DEVELOPING INSIGHTS WITH USERS AND CONSUMERS FURTHER DOWN THE CHAIN AND THEN USING THEM TO INFORM AND ENHANCE THE BUSINESS OF YOUR IMMEDIATE CUSTOMER ISN'T ARROGANT, IT'S CALLED PROACTIVITY"

CASE STUDY

MAGIC MIRRORS
Look Down the Chain

I heard a lovely example of Habit 7 – 'Look Down the Chain' which came from a very commoditised B2B market, that of cotton wash care labels.

Wash care labels are those tiny white tags that are attached to your clothes which tell you the composition of the fabric and how to wash and dry it. They are so utterly ubiquitous that you probably no longer register their existence at all. This would be the very definition of a B2B commodity on which so many neigh-sayers would already be bowing out of the Value Proposition process on the basis that nothing meaningful can be achieved.

The manufacturer of wash care labels in question wanted to create innovation within the market, and had developed tags with RFID technology which would allow the tags to interact and 'talk' to their environment. The problem was that initially the purchasing departments of the clothes manufacturers weren't interested. They couldn't see the value to them and they thought that the RFID technology was over-engineered, offering no tangible savings but clear on-cost to every item, which multiplied over hundreds of millions of garments made it highly unattractive.

The team at the wash care label company were focused on the left of the chain, the purchasers and payers, and needed to look down the chain for insight.

Eventually they started to proactively undertake their own market research into consumer habits within clothes retailers.

They looked down the chain and talked to the shop floor staff and the merchandisers to gather a new set of insights within the value chain.

The first thing that their research revealed was the habit for consumers to pick up items from a shelf with the intention of buying them, only to change their mind later and deposit the clothes onto the nearest rail or shelf.

What would be the likelihood of an item selling when it is out of position, away from the other sizes and similar designs? That's right, the answer is it won't sell. That store now has an orphan garment on its hands cluttering up its displays and with a negligible chance of ever being sold.

So the team were able to propose a solution for the purchasing department based on the shop floor experience of retail staff, essentially a handheld device that identifies those orphan items and helps staff return them efficiently to their proper location.

The next set of insights came from talking to shoppers, the end users of the clothes retailers.

What the market research discovered was that people don't visit the changing rooms within a clothes store more than once. Essentially, trying on clothes is a one-shot deal.

You collect up all the items you'd like to try on and eventually as a culmination of your shopping trip you head off to the undignified glory of the changing cubicles. Now if the jeans that you'd decided you liked happen to be a size too small, you don't go back out onto the shop floor and try the whole thing a second time. You abandon the exercise completely and head home with a mutter under your breath of "it wasn't meant to be."

The wash care label manufacturers proposed a solution called the Magic Mirror, which automatically reads the wash care label on the item as you enter the changing room. If for example you try on a pair of jeans in size 32 and they don't fit, the mirror shows more choices. Perhaps you'd like a size smaller, or a size bigger?

By simply tapping the new size on the screen, the assistant goes off to collect the correct size without you needing to abandon the cocoon of the changing room cubicle.

Perhaps you brought in a coat. The Mirror asks, "Did you know that the coat has a matching set of gloves, hat and scarf?" Tap the mirror and the assistant goes off to collect those from around the store.

By understanding the behaviour of end users, the team were able to re-frame the value of the RFID cloth label away from the cost of the technology, to the ROI of the upselling opportunity.

They could revisit the purchasing department with a genuine Value Proposition which shifted the paradigm away from the previous commodity story.

Whenever I hear B2B marketers lamenting the fact that their technology is commoditised and that insights and Value Propositions will not work for them I remind them that Coca-Cola is a commodity. It's essentially black sugary liquid which anyone could make. It's the active decision to transcend commoditisation that makes it happen and there are plenty of examples, from Gorilla Glass to Intel Chips to Bose Speakers to Gore-Tex fabric, where that has been a success.

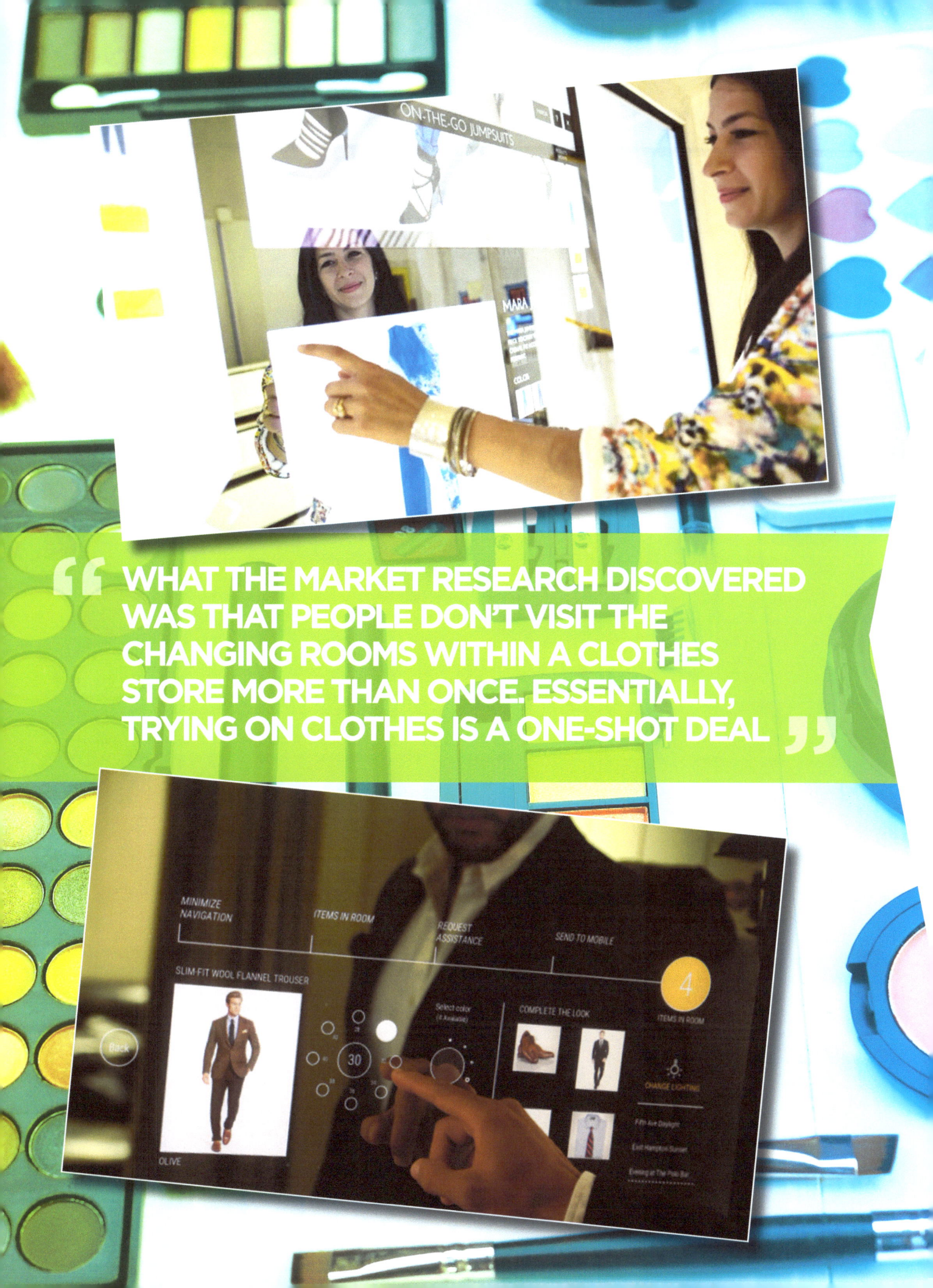

> "WHAT THE MARKET RESEARCH DISCOVERED WAS THAT PEOPLE DON'T VISIT THE CHANGING ROOMS WITHIN A CLOTHES STORE MORE THAN ONCE. ESSENTIALLY, TRYING ON CLOTHES IS A ONE-SHOT DEAL"

UBAMARKET

Look Down the Chain

I saw a cartoon recently in which the road sign on the way into a new town read: "Welcome to our Innovation Campus, where everything is the new Uber of something."

So, it was that my heart fell when I saw the name Ubamarket, presumably the new Uber of shopping? Where do these guys get their inspiration from for such thought-provoking names?

With a sense of trepidation I started looking into the Value Proposition of Ubamarket, intrigued by how the experience of the iconic taxi hailing service could be translated through semantic backflips into a relevant shopping app.

And here's the insight.

You know when you visit your local store and you need to find that small jar of pre-sliced beetroot in vinegar, but you don't know where it is located?

Wouldn't it be good if the exact location of that item was shown on your smartphone, like some exquisite beetroot homing device. You could navigate seamlessly through the aisles, by-passing the frozen vegetables, skirting the tins of passata and ending up exactly at the shelf you needed.

If you had a list of 12 items you needed to buy, you could enter them as a shopping list while at home or work, transfer them to the white-hot technology of your beetroot hunting smartphone, and then fly around your local Tesco without wasting a second.

Creating something like this is not as easy as it might first appear. As every store layout is different, the manufacturers of the app will need to essentially map every single convenience store in Britain. They will then need to enter the exact location of my beetroot slices in the app alongside every potential item and brand I might want to go shopping for. That's the small matter of 51,524 convenience stores and over 300,000 potential products.

Let's hope that no one moves the location of a product once it's been mapped! God forbid someone swaps the beetroot for gherkins in brine! I hate gherkins in brine.

Back to the Ubamarket concept for a second. How do we know it works? How can we be sure it will work for you in your time of need? Good news. The app has been piloted in the prestigious and doubtlessly complex setting of Warner's Budgens in Moreton in Marsh, Gloucestershire. You heard right.

Let's not dismiss Moreton in Marsh out of hand. In the last census there were 3,493 people living in this sleepy Cotswold village, the Budgens there is going to be hopping on market day!

Not one to avoid hyperbole, the maker of the shopping app which will rival Uber states that, "Ubamarket has evolved on a Darwinian scale (at warp speed) and has become the new way to shop faster and smarter whilst the retailer enjoys greater customer loyalty." Those guys in Moreton on Marsh are no pushovers you know! They can be hard to impress.

And it is at this point that I feel compelled to bring this story to its point. Why is this a bad example of a B2B innovation?

Well firstly, ask yourself why it's difficult to find things in a local store. Why is the milk and the bread and those essentials distributed so un-intuitively? Exactly to force shoppers to browse throughout the store, falling upon items that they previously had no intention of buying, such as gherkins in brine for example.

And who would be most disadvantaged by an app that took people directly to the items on their shopping list and only those items? Well, naturally, the retailer would suffer.

In an interview on the BBC I watched as the creator of the Ubamarket simultaneously pointed out this insight about the retailer and then in the same breath explained that his app would be funded by that exact same retailer.

In order to map all those stores, and fund the enormous investment in expanding Ubamarket at warp speed from the confines of Moreton in Marsh Budgens to your local high street, the retailers need to pay.

Except clearly they won't. There is no red thread. The consumer's need in this case and the retailer's need is diametrically opposed and the high likelihood is that even if this project could be funded despite retailers, the sheer scale of the task and investment required to realise the project means it's doomed.

By the way, thinking as always about the alternatives to Ubamarket. How about asking a shop assistant where the beetroot slices are? Too simple?

> "LET'S NOT DISMISS MORETON IN MARSH OUT OF HAND. IN THE LAST CENSUS THERE WERE 3,493 PEOPLE LIVING IN THIS SLEEPY COTSWOLD VILLAGE, THE BUDGENS THERE IS GOING TO BE HOPPING ON MARKET DAY!"

AND FINALLY...
Some More Heavenly Examples

When writing this book and researching the case studies, there were a couple of lovely examples that didn't quite make it into the full case studies but I felt you'd like to hear anyway.

Who doesn't like hearing more great examples of innovation done well?

Diamond Shreddies create new level of geometric superiority.

I often tell people on my training that you can use a new Value Proposition and insight to renovate an existing product and Diamond Shreddies is about the best example I've heard of a company doing just that. Without a single technical change to the underlying product Shreddies were able to create enormous news and positive feeling around the brand.

In case you don't know, Shreddies is a square breakfast cereal made by Kraft Foods and sold for over 70 years in the UK, Canada and New Zealand.

As part of a joke during a brainstorming session an intern suggested that they create a second variant of the product positioned as Diamond Shreddies. The leader of the Ogilvy and Mather creative team didn't dismiss the idea, she ran with it. Remember when people say there are no bad ideas in a brainstorm? Well some people mean it.

And Diamond Shreddies became a reality — it was just square Shreddies. Nothing had changed, the product was identical bar the packaging and the positioning. Consumers could now choose between the old square Shreddies or a pack of new improved diamond Shreddies. Believe it or not, there was even a "Combo Pack" that supposedly contained both versions.

Communication on the Shreddies website read: "Recent advances in cereal technology have allowed us to take Shreddies cereal to a whole new level of geometric superiority".

Did it work?

You bet.

Shreddies' market share leapt by nearly 20% and the beauty was that no one ever felt the need to patronise the consumer by explaining the joke. I guess this is the perfect example of Hiding the Hero (Heavenly Habit 5). The consumer got the gag, they felt cool for reading between the lines and the manufacturer credited them with being savvy.

Red Lightbulbs change the pecking order

I was in Hong Kong recently delivering a training course when one of the team relayed this lovely story to me about a big Dutch lightbulb manufacturer.

The story was that one of their employees was visiting a chicken farmer who explained the insight about how roosters tend to fight and peck each other to demonstrate superiority. That's where the phrase 'pecking order' comes from!

The rooster with the brightest red comb on the top of its head is considered to be dominant and the other roosters will ultimately attack it to take its place leading to injury, infection and loss of livestock for the farmer.

The answer? The company provided red lightbulbs to the chicken industry which made all the roosters' combs bright red and meant that it was impossible for any to appear dominant.

The attrition rate of roosters fell dramatically and the company went on to create a sizeable business selling what equated to red lightbulbs but with a far more attractive Value Proposition for many years afterwards.

Pig cannibalism leaves a nasty taste in the mouth

Along similar lines, I was training in Denmark where the enormous pig farming industry is so significant to the economy that there are 7 pigs for every person.

I heard a story about a company called Bitrex that makes a chemical that has the bitterest taste in the world. They use this in over 500 Value Propositions, from household bleaches to agro-chemicals. Essentially if you have an insight that something should not be eaten or put in your mouth, Bitrex is so disgusting that it makes you spit it out.

The story is that one of their employees discovered that pigs have an alarming habit of cannibalism, and they particularly like to bite each other's tails off, which often become infected leading to enormous costs for the farmer.

This small insight led to Bitrex creating a unique anti-tail biting solution for pigs. Even in B2B, companies can learn from insights and re-apply their existing technologies to create new and differentiated solutions.

THE 6 ELEMENTS METHOD

Don't let the success of your innovation come down to chance

Let me ask you a couple of quick questions:

How do you rate the chance of success of your current innovation?

Do you truly believe that your customer and not your technology is at the heart of your innovation?

When you ask your team what insight lies behind their ideas, how do they answer and do they really know what you are asking?

Do your teams employ a disciplined and robust method of creating an understanding of customer needs or is it more of a 'gut feel' approach?

Do you have more data than you know what to do with, but no breakthrough insights?

At the heart of all creative processes is discipline

You may not believe it, but many other functions think marketing isn't a discipline. They think that decisions are made on 'gut feel' alone and that there is no way to validate or structure the creative idea generation needed for innovation in a robust way.

I disagree.

For over a decade I have been teaching Value Proposition creation using a simple 6 block thinking framework. It wasn't something I invented, as it's built on 60 years of industry best practice, but I have refined and perfected it for use in large complex organisations. I've expanded the methodology to encapsulate the culture of technology and R&D driven organisations and for use in complex B2B environments too.

My framework has now been stress tested and proven to work in these multistakeholder B2B environments as well as B2C; it's been used to launch products, services and brands alike.

My approach has been used to develop new products, improve existing ones and reposition those that were well established in the market. Put simply, my approach works.

It's not rocket science or witchcraft

The world's best marketing companies have known for years that to tell a story of a product, service or brand you need to use the same 6 core elements.

You need to focus on a target, work out what they need, then see why other alternatives fail to address that opportunity adequately.

Anything complicated or contentious so far?

Then you need to clearly communicate the benefit you offer, and prove you can deliver it in a better way than those others.

Communicating your ideas inside and outside the company in a proposition that follows that structure is proven to work every time.

So that's what I teach.

I don't overcomplicate it, wrap it up in jargon or try and add stuff to make myself seem clever. What I do, however, is explain it really simply and give rich and elegant examples at every turn. I find people learn better that way.

My philosophy at Outside In™ is "Seeing and Doing is Believing."

I know that insight driven innovation and Value Proposition creation may not have been the historical culture of my clients. I regularly meet and consult with highly intelligent people who need persuading that such a shift is appropriate for them or possible given the established culture of their organisation. Sometimes I meet people who think they already know everything about insights, but haven't challenged their thinking or updated their skills in years.

Smart people need persuading to change

As a result I build all my methods on a series of case studies close to the day to day situation of my clients. I prove through showing example after example that the move to insight driven innovation is not only achievable but highly desirable for those I train.

This constantly evolving use of up to date products and examples to illustrate my learning objectives prevents my Outside In ™ workshops becoming reliant on dry theory and keeps them interactive and engaging.

That's why my workshops have such unprecedented word of mouth recommendation and have been proven to change the culture of huge established companies where others had failed.

ABOUT MAT SHORE
The man...

Mat has an infectious passion for innovation. His ability to explain and encourage new thinking in innovation has led to him being invited to train thousands of people in North America, Latin America, Africa, Asia and Europe over the last 11 years.

His material on innovation has been delivered to over 35,000 people worldwide. He has refined and championed a 6 block Value Proposition approach that is so simple and intuitive to use that it's now best practice in companies with a combined turnover of $150 billion worldwide.

This focus on making Value Proposition and insight writing accessible has led to Mat developing technology of his own. His Proposition Engine software actually helps teams master the skill of writing and capturing great insights and product concepts.

In 2013 Mat was asked to be the keynote speaker at the PMA conference in New Orleans, one of the world's largest conferences with 20,000 attendees. In this speech he delivered his 7 Deadly Sins speech to great acclaim. You can see a clip from his keynote on his website: matshore.com.

Mat's unique humour and irreverence means his weekly blog on topical innovation success and failure is viewed by thousands. His opinion is also regularly sought by business publications and newspapers. In 2015 Mat was interviewed by The Times on his thoughts about bad innovation and how he would improve the quality.

In 2003 Mat founded Outside In™, a successful innovation and training company which helps clients worldwide challenge their preconceived ideas on insights, propositions and innovation. In the last 11 years, Outside In have consulted on B2B and B2C innovations in 27 countries.. As a result Mat has one or two frequent flyer miles.

Mat has worked on countless innovation projects with market leaders such as GE, Philips, Citrix, Electrolux, Samsung, Lafarge, Carestream, AON, Belkin, Gemalto and Analogic. He has also worked with service providers, agencies, universities and start-ups. Mat's extensive expertise in this area led to him being asked to train the MBA faculty at Washington University in insight and proposition development.

Apart from his training and public speaking talents, Mat has many years' experience actually running live innovation projects.

In his career Mat has worked across diverse markets, from launching new coffee machines to neonatal MRI scanners. He is a world leading expert in synthesising insights, generating propositions and moderating customer and consumer work.

However it is Mat's humour and ability to transfer knowledge to marketers and engineers alike that makes him so successful. As a leading authority in coaching and developing innovation, he'll always find a relevant and motivating example to inspire your team to new breakthrough thinking.

Subscribe to Mat's YouTube channel – MatShoreInnovation, or follow him on LinkedIn for up to date case studies.

Mat Shore
Marketing Consultant

BOOKING OUTSIDE IN

We get it! Creating compelling new ideas and explaining their value is tough.

Outside In™ are global experts in teaching the competency of insight and Value Proposition (product concept) creation in B2B and B2C organisations. Our success is reflected in the fact that in 2015 our tools and thinking are used by over 250,000 employees around the world.

Because we specialise in just this one topic, our expertise has been sought in the boardrooms of global multinationals such as Philips, GE, Citrix and Samsung.

We have delivered training to 35,000 people in 27 countries across a diverse range of B2B, B2C, Service and Product companies. Teams have joined us from blue chip companies like Glaxo, Unilever, Lafarge, Electrolux and Nestle. We have also been asked to train smaller organisations and incubators, start-ups and university faculties. Maybe we have trained you in the past, or maybe you are part of a new team who have yet to experience our training?

The profile of trainees for Outside In's session normally comprise of a mix of upstream and downstream marketing and sales folks, market research professionals, senior business heads, business group managers, product managers and R&D (Product Engineers and Developers).

What does our training cover?

We train teams in the following:

1. The reason why consumer/customer insight is key to success.
2. The true definition of an insight and how to avoid the common traps and misconceptions.
3. Where and how to generate better insights.
4. How to create insights in a complex B2B stakeholder chain.
5. How to validate whether your insights are fresh, relevant and powerful.
6. How to turn those insights into winning Value Propositions (Concepts).
7. How to ensure your Value Proposition is clear and differentiated.
8. How to make sure your winning Value Proposition drives all subsequent company activity from Design, R&D and Communication to Sales and Claims Support.
9. How the best companies deploy this thinking through their business to get it to stick even despite initial resistance or conflicting cultures.
10. What are the best tools to use to make all this simple and intuitive.

What Format does the training come in?

1. Foundation Training - All the core elements in 2 days of training – up to 20 participants can attend in every session.
2. Advanced Training – Advanced insight generation and research methods, claims generation and more.
3. Become a VP coach / Masterclass – Enhance the skills and tools of your internal experts.

Do we do coaching and workshops to solve live projects?

1. Project Clinics – 1 day workshop to sort out the strategy and clean up those sticky projects lacking an insight or a tight, differentiated proposition.
2. Kick Start Workshop - Launch the whole team in the same direction on those key new projects that need energy and inspiration in just one day.
3. Remote Coaching Subscription – After your training, have us on call to support your team by phone, with monthly case studies, or a series of virtual meetings on an ongoing basis.
4. Proposition Engine –Our interactive software for creating value propositions and helping write all the associated discussion guides, advertising, sales and R&D briefs.

How should I get in touch?
Call +44 7961 969997 or email Mat@OutsideInCompany.com

JARGON BUSTER
Mat's Innovation Dictionary

When I first started consulting with big clients I realised quickly that although people threw around terminology and jargon about innovation freely, most were not really sure about the definition of the words they were using. Words like insight, Value Proposition and disruption are possibly the most overused and misunderstood terms in business.

I started to create an innovation dictionary of terms which would help my clients and standardise the understanding of these buzzwords. Some of these terms appear in this book, so I've captured a few of the key definitions below. Enjoy!

Insight – A discovery about the customer or consumers unmet needs that was previously unknown and creates a competitive advantage in creating a more relevant solution.

See 'What is an insight?' on YouTube MatShoreInnovation channel for more details.

Insight Formula – (The 3 W's) - An insight must contain the following:

   What does the consumer do now? (Observation)
   Why do they do that? (Motivation)
   Wow no one has ever said that before! (Deeper understanding)

Insight written structure – The standard best practice way to write down an insight:

   Situation – What is the target doing now? (Describe them and their context)
   Dilemma – What is the barrier, friction or trade off creating their priority problem?
   Perfect Situation – What is their desired outcome?

See 'Writing an Insight Video' on YouTube MatShoreInnovation channel for more details.

Observation – A fact, statistic or Data Point about what the customer or market is doing. The start point or building blocks of an insight, but lacking a competitive deeper understanding of the underlying behaviour.

See 'Insights vs Observations – Video Tutorial' on YouTube MatShoreInnovation channel for more details.

Accepted Customer Belief (ACB) – A consumer prejudice about your market, need or brand which prevents the target group from articulating their true desired outcome. Often ingrained over time and difficult to reverse in mature markets. Also known as Accepted Consumer Belief.

Industry Perpetuated Myth (IPM) – A statistic, feature or attribute that is falsely escalated in importance by the industry to their own advantage. These eventually lead to specification wars and customers focusing on unhelpful and irrelevant functionality even once the attribute has achieved a point of maximum utility.(think blades on a razor or CT Slice Wars).

Target – The person for whom your proposition should be first choice.

Consumer – The person who consumes our solution day to day but not always the purchase decision maker.

Customer – The person or organisation that we sell our solution through.

Stakeholder – A key group or individual in our value chain that can make or break the success of innovation.

Value Chain – A list of every stakeholder between us and the end user.

See 'Child in an MRI – Example' on YouTube MatShoreInnovation channel for more details.

End User – Last person in the value chain to experience the solution. Often can be the Consumer.

Disruptive Innovation – A solution which solves an unmet need that no competitors have addressed. Does not have to be a new technology, but can be the re-application of an existing technology in a new way.

Incremental Innovation – A step forward in the optimisation of an existing technology or method.

Renovation Innovation – The repackaging or re-positioning of an existing solution without major changes to its design or technology.

Value Proposition – A Value Proposition is a clear story that explains how your product or service solves a customer's problem in a unique or superior way. See 'How to write a Value Proposition' on YouTube MatShoreInnovation channel for more details.

6 Elements of a Value Proposition – The thinking framework required to structure a Value Proposition. These elements are present in most large marketing companies' tools and methods.

Brand Positioning – A form of words or document used in marketing communication that capture how the higher-level Value Proposition will translate to messaging.

Elevator Pitch – A short pithy couple of lines that sum up the idea or strategy to internal or external stakeholders before the doors of the elevator open (less than 30 seconds).

Alternatives – Other ways the target can solve the insight.

Benefit – The promise to solve the insight both functionally and emotionally.

See 'Defining your Benefit – So What test!' on YouTube MatShoreInnovation channel for more details.

Reasons to Believe – Proof points and Endorsements that our solution will deliver the benefit.

Superiority – What makes our solution discriminated or unique compared to the alternatives (Also known as Unique Selling Point - USP).

Claim – The legally supportable form of words that communicates our superiority to the target.

Tag Line – Succinct form of words that express the offer in advertising (also known as Strap Line).

Insight Validation – Market research to qualify or quantify that our insight is true and clear.

Insight Confrontation – Market research in which competing written insight hypotheses are shown to the target and compared, refined and ranked.

Concept Testing – The testing and validation of a written Value Proposition with the target.

See 'How to test a Value Proposition' on YouTube MatShoreInnovation channel for more details.

Value – A subjective measure of why the benefit matters to the target or stakeholder (not the same as Price).

Price – An objective cost to purchase put on a solution (not the same as Value).

Technology Push – The desire to create needs around a predefined solution.

Feature – An aspect of what the solution does for inclusion in the Reasons to Believe (also known as Attribute).

Specification – Quantified value of a given Feature.

Red Thread – Validation that all stakeholders see value in the same need being addressed.

Segmentation – The division of the target into smaller subsets based on common attributes such as age, geography or attitudes and needs.

The 5 Whys – Commonly used tool in Design For 6 Sigma (a quality control methodology) for diving into customers' underlying beliefs and needs.

Maslow's Hierarchy of Needs – A theory created in 1943 which expounds how people value emotional and spiritual benefits more than basic rational ones.

Insight Driven – The desire to create solutions around unmet needs.

Marketing – The ability to add value to a solution beyond its cost of creation by better understanding the needs of the target.

Off Strategy – A solution that deviates from the agreed strategy or Value Proposition.

Credibility Gap – The lack of belief amongst the target that a benefit can be delivered or lack of understanding of how that might be achieved in practice.

Brand – A top line commitment of what a solution or company will deliver over time.

Logo – A visual identity that represents the brand.

Advertising – The process of communicating the company's product or service in association with the brand.

7 DEADLY SINS BOOK

Mat Shore's companion book to 'The 7 Heavenly Habits' is entitled 'The 7 Deadly Sins of Innovation' and is now available to buy. It contains numerous hysterical examples of innovation sins and lots of elegant examples of innovation saints. Based on his popular presentations and training sessions that Mat has delivered to 35,000 people around the world, 'The 7 Deadly Sins of Innovation' is the most entertaining and enlightening book you are likely to read this year.

To order the book just visit - Matshore.com

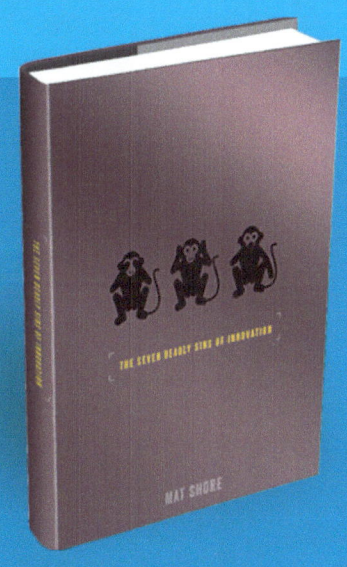

Notes...

www.ingramcontent.com/pod-product-compliance
Lightning Source LLC
Chambersburg PA
CBHW051210220526
45473CB00003B/971